What coaches said about our first edition

"This book is an excellent resource for coaches. It's more than a book of drills. It describes how kids can master the necessary skills. I found this to be more helpful than coaching clinics. I wish I had this book three years ago."

"This book could be called *Soccer 101*. . . . It's a great place to start if you have four- to six-year-old children. It shows you how to teach the basics and how to keep them interested in the game. Good for a first-time coach or those of us who have not coached the first-time soccer player."

"This is a very good, basic book for the parent wishing to start coaching youth soccer at the earliest level. The book assumes no prior knowledge of the sport. This is a good book for the parent who's going out on the field to coach for the first time or who wants to understand and enjoy the game more fully."

"This is a great book to read when you first start coaching a team of five-, six-, or seven-year-olds. It has right level of drills and tactics for those ages. I've lent it out several times to friends who are just getting started as coaches. It has the rules of soccer and guidelines for putting together a practice. It also has good, basic drills that are easy to set up and that teach the fundamental tactics of soccer. I especially liked the way it shows how to teach heading and shooting. I recommend it for a first-time coach."

"I run a kid's team (under twelves), and this book has helped me with ideas for training sessions. It is well written and practical."

"This book is great! I coach eleven-year-old girls and use the book every practice. It gives useful drills but also gives tips for being a good coach."

COACHING

JIM SAN MARCO
AND
KURT ASCHERMANN

FOREWORD BY TONY DICICCO,
FORMER HEAD COACH OF U.S. WOMEN'S NATIONAL
SOCCER TEAM, 1996 OLYMPIC GOLD MEDAL WINNERS,
1999 FIFA WORLD CUP CHAMPIONS

NEW PHOTOGRAPHS BY
MARIO PARTENOPE

KIDS
TO PLAY
SOCCER

A FIRESIDE BOOK
PUBLISHED BY SIMON & SCHUSTER
NEW YORK LONDON TORONTO SYDNEY

We would like to thank our soccer players whose pictures appear throughout the book:

Jennifer Aschermann   Kira Pancotti
Kurt Aschermann   Geoff Simone
Kristin Aschermann   Ali Vitali
Mary San Marco   Alyssa Vitali
Jill San Marco   Amy Wagner

Permission to reprint USSF soccer rules courtesy of FIFA

Glossary terms and definitions used by permission of the Ontario Soccer Association—from their *Schools Programme Manual*.

Fireside
A Division of Simon & Schuster, Inc.
1230 Avenue of the Americas
New York, NY 10020

Designed by Mary Austin Speaker

Manufactured in the United States of America

10   9   8   7   6   5   4   3   2   1

The Library of Congress has cataloged the previous edition as follows:
San Marco, Jim.
    Coaching kids to play soccer / Jim San Marco and Kurt Aschermann ;
foreword by Julio Mazzei.
        p.   cm.
    "A Fireside book."
    Includes bibliography.
    1. Soccer for children—Coaching.   I. Aschermann, Kurt.   II. Title.
GV943.8 .S26 1987
796.334'024054—dc19   87008544

For information about special discounts for bulk purchases,
please contact Simon & Schuster Special Sales at
1-800-456-6798 or business@simonandschuster.com.

ISBN-13: 978-1-4165-4672-6
ISBN-10:   1-4165-4672-3

This book is dedicated to: Lou Gallo and Frank Chillemi, who started my soccer life; Mario and Ann, my parents, who gave me my life; Skip, Johnny, Deb, and Fran, who have been such a big part of my life; Lesley, my wife, who has with great love and patience shared my life; Mary and Jill, my children, who each day help me to appreciate life; and finally, to God, the most important thing in my life.

—JIM SAN MARCO

This book is dedicated to my children—Jennifer, Kurt, and Kristin—who I had the pleasure of coaching as they were growing up. My coaching seems to have worked. They are good athletes and, more important, are also good people. I also want to say thanks to my father and brother for always being there for me, on the field and off. And to Cynthia, thanks for putting up with me even though I lied and said I didn't like sports.

—KURT ASCHERMANN

CONTENTS

FOREWORD

Soccer is still a youth sport phenomenon, with the numbers of players continuing to grow and more and more children and parents being introduced to the beautiful game. *Coaching Kids to Play Soccer* is a valuable and necessary tool for any player, coach, or parent. Jim San Marco and Kurt Aschermann have captured what every parent and coach needs to know as they launch their children, themselves, and their families into the youth soccer experience.

I was fortunate to coach at the highest level and watched my national team win an Olympic Gold Medal in 1996 and a World Cup championship in 1999. Even with players like Mia Hamm, Michelle Akers, Julie Foudy, Kristine Lilly, Briana Scurry, and others, the key ingredient to success is fun. If soccer is fun, players will train with that extra effort and their game will continually improve. Without fun, the joy of the game disappears and, with it, player development. *Coaching Kids to Play Soccer* addresses how to keep the fun in the game; how to tell when there's too much soccer; how, as a parent, you can motivate your child to train on his or her own; and how, as a parent, you can keep your child's and your own soccer experience positive.

The days when soccer was considered a foreign game are long gone—the media that still see it that way have been passed by—but the cultural exchanges and learning from different people from around the globe that soccer offers is special. *Coaching Kids to Play*

Soccer gives us just the right balance for the young player and will be a welcome addition to anyone's soccer library. Enjoy!

TONY DiCICCO
president, SoccerPlus Camps
technical director of FSA SoccerPlus FC
former head coach, USA Women's National Soccer Team

PREFACE

Just how many kids are there in America playing soccer? Estimates vary, but the quantified analysis is really irrelevant. Suffice it to say there are *lots* of kids playing the game the rest of the world calls football. An afternoon's ride through Long Island in New York, or the suburbs of St. Louis or Los Angeles, will prove the point. One can see youngsters of every shape, size, color, and sex kicking that round thing from one end of a field to the other.

The proponents of soccer development in the United States will tell you it's an American game because all kinds of people live here and anyone can play soccer. Others contend that the game takes no skill—it's just a bunch of kids kicking each other's shins.

The purpose of this book is *not* to try to convince anyone of anything. We want to state, however, that we fall into the first category—we love the sport of soccer, we see what it's done for millions of kids, and we want to see its continued growth. But we also believe that soccer people spend too much time *preaching* the virtues of the sport and not enough time *teaching* them. They need to abandon the argument altogether and get on with the sport's development.

A point often made pertaining to soccer is: with so many kids playing it, how come you can't get them to watch it played professionally? We have some thoughts on the matter, but, quite frankly, we don't lose sleep over it. You won't find the answer to that question in this book.

This book, then, is simply to help the volunteer or first-time coach learn the game and advise how best to teach it. It is written as if that person knows nothing at all about soccer (a safe bet, in some cases). Certainly, veteran coaches will also find this book informative. It will most likely reinforce many of the important soccer concepts you are stressing to your team now. At the same time, coaches will find in this book various coaching concepts they may have not seen or read before.

In 1984, Kurt Aschermann coauthored a very successful baseball instructional book titled *Coaching Kids to Play Baseball and Softball*, a companion to this book. The preface said, "This book is for you, the volunteer coach or parent who loves the game of baseball and enjoys working with youngsters, but may need some assistance in teaching the sport effectively and enjoyably. It's a book of basics, not a detailed skill level book."

This book, *Coaching Kids to Play Soccer*, is the same type of manual. We have combined our administrative, coaching, and soccer experience into a guidebook for the volunteer coach. You won't find esoteric descriptions of elaborate defenses and strategy in these pages. What you *will* find is all the information you need to coach the likes of second-grade Kipp's Pharmacy Raiders, a fourteen-year-old select team, or a junior varsity squad at your local high school, and thus enjoy with them what is truly the world's most popular sport.

The authors come from different backgrounds. Kurt Aschermann is currently president and COO of Charity Partners, LLC. Though Aschermann was a high-school baseball coach for five years, he has only a little experience coaching soccer, serving principally as a coach for five-, six-, and seven-year-olds. He has extensive youth sports experience and is considered an expert in the field of volunteer youth athletics.

Jim San Marco, a past president of the Westchester County Soccer Coaches Association, is one of the most successful high-school soccer coaches in New York State. His Edgemont High School (Westchester, New York) soccer teams won numerous league and sectional cups, and his combined record in eighteen years of coaching is an incredible 211-67-24. He has served as a New York State soccer clinician to certify youth coaches, presented at the New York State Physical Education Convention and soccer clinics throughout the New York, New Jersey, and Connecticut metropolitan areas. He has also traveled with youth groups to Europe and coached in the North American Junior Maccabi Games.

COACHING KIDS TO PLAY SOCCER

1
IT'S ALL YOURS, COACH

A simple, important, sobering fact needs to be stated at the outset: as a youth soccer coach you have a huge responsibility to everyone on the team. Not only do these youngsters want to learn soccer from you, but they also want to win, want to score some goals—and they don't want to be yelled at. Your impact in the game is rivaled only by that of the parent, and, in certain circumstances, it surpasses that influence. You will find that your kids want to please you more than anyone else, and this simple fact can place tremendous pressure on you. It should guide your every action.

We believe that your responsibilities as a youth soccer coach are easily stated:

Fun
Learning
Individual development
Winning

... *in that order!* Let's look at each one in turn.

Fun: It may come as a surprise to some of the parents of the players, but 99 percent of their kids are playing soccer because they want to have fun playing it. Those kids in your charge, Coach, have joined the league and your team to enjoy themselves. The minute you lose sight of that as your principal motivating factor, you're in trouble.

Learning: Twenty years ago we said youth league soccer coaches had further to go than youth league coaches in other sports because we didn't know this game! We said players' and coaches' ignorance meant coaches had more work to do to learn the game. That isn't nearly as true today as then—soccer is part of physical education programs now, and most colleges have teams. But though PE teachers are taught how to coach soccer, most adult coaches still need to know the game to make sure their players learn. To us, learning is the second most important responsibility of the youth league coach. The days of the uninformed soccer coach throwing out the ball to scrimmage and calling it a practice are over. Your goal is to make your players into students of the game and help them learn all they can about this great sport.

Individual Development: A nine-year-old should be compared with himself, not every other nine-year-old. You help a team develop by helping each individual. And if you've succeeded in helping most of your athletes become better soccer players by the last week of the season, you're a winning coach, regardless of your record.

Winning: We believe the outcome of the game yields winners and learners—there are no losers. Winning is important and needs to be an important part of the development of soccer players. But perspective becomes the important consideration, because while winning is important and must be part of the education process of an athlete, it needs to be understood as the result of hard work and individual development. The coach who succeeds in teaching the sport—individually and to a group—will find success in the won/lost column. The coach who helps the team keep winning or losing in perspective will find success in the personal development column.

THE BALL STOPS HERE

Coaches in volunteer leagues are often acquired like goalies: no one wants to do the job, so someone gets drafted. You may have come to your soccer duties purely out of love for the sport or, like many, out of love for your child. Any coach, regardless of experience, though, has to have knowledge of the sport and the ability to impart that knowledge to the kids. If you have come to your soccer team because your child wanted to play and no one else was there to teach or lead the team, how you deal with these two issues may well determine if the players have a positive or a negative experience.

2

GENERAL GUIDELINES FOR PARENTS, PLAYERS, AND COACHES

As in any group activity, stating clearly what is and is not acceptable behavior for parents and players is a good way to start. The group—in this case, your team—should understand the philosophy of the league and team.

The following are some basic, commonsense thoughts for parents, players, and coaches about to become involved in youth soccer. You may want to copy these and pass them out at your first team meeting.

PARENTS

1. The primary reason children play is to have fun, not so much to win or to be with their friends.

2. Your child should play fairly, within the rules of the game.

3. You should help the coaches in any way possible. Remember, they're volunteers and usually parents, too.

4. Don't make negative comments to any child, especially your own. Understand that when one of the players makes a mistake, he didn't do it on purpose; your method of correction should reflect that.

5. You should praise the effort of every player; remember, the lesser-skilled players are just as important as the superstars.

6. Be a parent who leads by example. Don't say one thing and do another.

PLAYERS

1. Always play fairly within the rules.

2. Maintain poise under difficult conditions. It's very easy to maintain composure when things go right; when they don't, real athletes step forward and stand up to the test.

3. Control your emotions, even if you feel your opponent is playing unfairly.

4. Support and encourage your teammates at all times. Any mistakes they make are surely not done on purpose.

5. Play as hard as you can in practice and games. Don't let your teammates down because of your lack of effort.

6. Show respect to your coaches and referees. Without them you would not be playing the game.

COACHES

1. Kids play soccer to have fun, so any decision you make concerning them should reflect that.

2. Be a knowledgeable coach. Read about soccer, discuss soccer with other coaches, go to clinics. You must know what you're talking about.

3. Demand that your players play within the rules of the game. If they win dishonestly, they haven't won at all.

4. Set a positive example for your players. Respect isn't given to anyone; it must be earned.

5. The safety of your players must be a priority. Don't take chances with their health or well-being. Winning the game means little when compared to overall safety.

6. Respect the opposing team and the referees, whether you approve of their actions or not.

3
PRACTICE PREPARATION (What Do I Do First?)

Planning the first practice session requires you to assure that the proper tone is set and that you accomplish your objectives (let alone control the troops!).

After you have received a roster of the players, it's a good idea to send a letter to parents explaining your views of soccer in general terms. Let them know what you will be doing at practices and in games. Mention immediately what you expect from them and the children. In this way, no one will be surprised by anything that occurs during the season.

Your letter should include (1) what each player needs to bring to the first practice; (2) when practice will take place and how long it will last; (3) a practice schedule, as well as a game schedule, to accommodate any long-range plans (including scheduling conflicts that might result in a player missing a practice or a game); (4) a phone chain and refreshment schedule for the team; and (5) some information about yourself—your background, family information, and soccer experience.

A sample letter follows.

Dear Parents:

Welcome to the Juniors' Soccer Program! We begin playing on Saturday, September 20, at the old middle school field. Practices will be on Saturdays from September 20 through November 1, from ten to eleven o'clock.

We will not be traveling and competing against other communities. Instead, our playing will be geared toward having FUN, taking fruit-punch breaks, socializing with kindergarten friends, chasing butterflies, and, if our children will cooperate a little, learning about the game of soccer. As parents, we are well aware of the attention spans and physical limitations of our children. This program is not about to make polished soccer players out of four- and five-year-olds. First, it would be impossible, and second, it would be a frustrating situation for everyone if we tried to do that. Instead, it is my hope that the kids will have fun, become a bit more fit, and learn about themselves and others as they play together. I hope to accomplish these things through the game of soccer. We will be instructing the children in the basic rules of the game and the fundamental skills of the sport as we try to reach our goals.

The following are some important things you should know:

1. Your child may wear sneakers or cleats, and we require that he also wear shin guards.
2. We will be using a size 3 soccer ball, smaller than the official size 5, which will put less strain on players' legs. Purchasing a size 3 ball would prove a worthy investment for your child. Please try to bring a ball (with your name on it) to practice. We will do some exercises where each youngster will need a ball.
3. Please be prompt when dropping off or picking up your child at the practices. Practice will last for one hour only.
4. If your child wears eyeglasses, be certain that the lenses are shatterproof or plastic. If they are not, have your child wear an eyeglass protective mask.
5. I have asked a few parents to help serve in a telephone chain in case inclement weather causes us to cancel a practice or a game. If there is any doubt in your mind and you have not been called, just contact me at 123-4567.
6. Seven parents have volunteered to coach our children. We encourage you to join us at our practices, to help or just to watch. The more assistance we have at each practice, the more individual attention each

child will receive. If you learn the skills and drills, do them with your child at home—think how much faster she will learn. And you, too, will have fun!

Please call me if you have any questions or comments.

Thanks in advance,
Coach Smith

TELEPHONE CHAIN

CAPTAINS

Joe Smith	123-4567	will call	Mary Jones	890-1234
			Ann Smith	567-8901
John Doe	234-5678	will call	Sue Johnson	901-2345
			Jane Hansen	678-9012
Lynn James	345-6789	will call	Ann S. John	012-3456
			Bill Joseph	789-0123
Mary Mason	456-7890	will call	Bob Johns	123-4567
			Sue Jones	890-1234
Jane Deer	567-8901	will call	Alice Smith	234-5678
			Ann Winters	901-2345
Wanda Simke	678-9012	will call	Al Frump	345-6789
			Sue Stein	012-3456
Al Lance	789-0123	will call	Jeff Jones	476-7890
			Jean James	123-4567

COACH SMITH will make the initial call to the captains to start the chain.

JOE SHOE has been kind enough to organize the water and punch-break schedule. PLEASE DO YOUR PART TO HELP.

PRACTICE SCHEDULE:

SATURDAYS ONLY, 10:00 A.M. TO 11:00 A.M.

September	20
September	27
October	4
October	11
October	18
October	25
November	1

On the first day of practice you should be at least fifteen to twenty minutes early, allowing you time to check for any problems with the field or anything else, and to try to resolve them. (You'd be surprised at some of the things first-time coaches have found on day one!)

Set up equipment for your first practice exercise beforehand. This will save time later on. As the players and parents arrive, welcome them and introduce yourself. The parents, remember, are leaving a prized possession with you; they deserve to meet you right away. Ask parents to stay together so you can have a short team meeting before practice begins. Briefly state your expectations of the players and the scheduled season, touching on how you hope to meet these expectations if they will do their best, help one another, never give up competing, and so forth.

After you talk, loosen up your players with *running and stretching* as you start practice. You will have quite a few appropriate exercises to use after reading this book.

As practice gets under way, you will begin a mental evaluation of the players in order to help determine what particular practice is needed most. The evaluation sheet shown on page 13 will help you assess each player's strengths and weaknesses. Obviously, it's a tool. You may or may not want to share it with the individual players, (and, frankly, sharing it with parents could be risky. You'd be surprised at how a parent's analysis of his or her child's ability often differs from reality! You might be better off asking parents to evaluate their children first. Then you can make suggestions for improvement.)

As part of your preparation for the first practice, it is important for you to have a working knowledge of first-aid procedures. Any vigorous activity increases the possibility of injury, so it's imperative that you do everything you can to ensure the safety of your players. A first-aid course, which can usually be taken in one day and is offered by most league and recreation departments, is strongly recommended. (In many states, such a course is mandatory in order to coach a high-school team.) The time spent learning proper procedures is just as important as the time taken to read this book. Do it—you won't regret it.

CONDUCTING A MEANINGFUL PRACTICE

Trust us on this one, Coach: **There is nothing more boring in the entire world of sport than a poorly planned and run practice.** You can literally waste the entire practice time if you don't know what you're going to do every minute *before* you get there.

There are some simple rules to follow when planning your practices that we feel guarantee your time with your players will be quality time:

1. **Never try to do too much.** If you try to put in your offense, defense, and goal-kick strategy on the same day, you will succeed only in confusing your players.

2. **Teach one skill at a time.** It's hard enough for little folks to understand one skill at a time. If you try to do more than one, you might just be doing too much.

3. **You must be able to demonstrate the new skill even in slow motion.** If you aren't skilled enough to actually show what you mean, you must have someone on hand who is.

4. **After you've taught it, try it.** Many coaches teach a skill, then move on to another. Try it while it's still fresh in mind.

5. **After trying it, add some pressure.** It's always a good idea to let your players try a new skill with someone trying to stop them. GAME-RELATED PRESSURE, which obviously better approximates what they will feel in a contest, can be added as proficiency increases.

6. **After teaching and trying, review it again.** Reinforcement is important. The best time to do that is right after you have spent time on the skill.

7. **Make it fun, fast-paced, and frequently changed.** Practice *has to be fun* or you won't accomplish much. By changing the activities and keeping things moving, you will find less boredom in the ranks, and more learning.

A SAMPLE PRACTICE OUTLINE

Though no two practice sessions will be exactly alike, they should all be structured basically the same. Following is a general outline, which details the steps to take for meaningful practice:

1. Start with a meeting at which you explain what you will do that day. It's also a good time to talk about past practices or even a game just played.

2. Warm up your team. (See Chapter 15.)

3. Teach new skills first. The best time for learning is when players are freshest and the most eager. That's at the start of practice.

4. Do TSTTT:

T   *Teach it*—explain the skill

S   *Show it*—demonstrate the skill

T   *Try it*—let the players do the skill *without* pressure

T   *Test it*—let the players do the skill *with* pressure

T   *Try it*—review the skill

5. Finish each practice with another meeting. Review what you've just accomplished and talk about what is coming up. The next game or practice schedule should be touched on at this time, too, as well as anything else you want your players to remember. It's a good idea to bring the parents in on this one.

SUMMARY

The well-organized and well-run practice is essential to a good soccer program. The little time you take to *prepare* will be well worth your while in the long run.

PLAYER SKILL EVALUATION SHEET

If you had just received a promotion and were moving into a new office as boss, you would quickly evaluate the talent or skills of your employees. As a soccer coach you must do likewise with your players.

After a few practices with the kids, sit down with your assistant coaches and evaluate the players. Mark down what you perceive to be their weaknesses and strengths. This will help you set individual and team goals. Each practice should provide all players with a chance to work on their weaknesses. At the end of the season, reevaluate your players; show them how they have improved and where you think they can improve more.

The form opposite provides a simple recording and evaluation system:

CODE:
1—Skilled player
2—Player has some skill
3—Player has little skill

One thing separates soccer from almost all other sports: running—as in, constant running. In our game, many players, including the goalie, spend a lot of time running. This may surprise you, Coach, but most kids don't know how to run. Oh, they know how to get from one place to another quickly, but we guarantee that most of them have poor mechanics in their running style. We believe that evaluating how they run before you start your season, then working on improving the mechanics of running, will pay off in the long run.

Here are the things you want to look for in running style:

1. Elbows should be close to the body while the arms are pumping. Elbows that fly add unneeded movement that will slow the body down.

2. Knees should be brought straight up, causing the thighs to be parallel to the ground. Feet and thighs can fly away from the body, causing extra wind resistance and a slowed-down player.

3. Hands and legs should be pumped vigorously when running. The most important thing is to teach your players to stay relaxed, especially from the shoulders to the fingers. Don't let them raise their shoulders. Keep them loose. A great suggestion to help them stay relaxed is to have your players pretend to hold a potato chip between their thumb and index finger while running. If they can run without breaking a potato chip, they are relaxed.

4. Players should lean slightly forward when running. (Sprinters lean forward when they run.)

5. Lateral movement is important to the game and must be evaluated and taught as well. Remember, kids move sideways in sports almost as much as forward and backward.

PLAYER EVALUATION FORM

NAME	PASSING	SHOOTING	RECEIVING	HEADING	DRIBBLING	SPEED/ AGILITY	COMMENTS

6. The ability to run backward is also important in soccer. It, too, must be evaluated and taught.

You may want to add a small line on your evaluation sheet where you can indicate which players need work on movement. But remember, all players need to work on movement, and it should be part of your practices.

4
TEN IMPORTANT THINGS YOUR PLAYERS AND PARENTS SHOULD KNOW

As we state frequently in this book, we believe strongly that to be a good coach it is essential to communicate well with players and their parents. Before you start your season, we suggest you copy these important maxims and share them with your team. These simple guidelines will help you clearly explain to your players what is expected of them. We also think they set a tone for the kind of play you expect.

Take time to go through the maxims individually. Refer to them often during the season. You will find pretty soon that your players will start referring to them, too.

1. A good player needs skills, conditioning, and knowledge. To be the best you can be, you need all three. No matter what position you play, you still need to be in shape and be able to head, pass, receive, shoot, make space, and play defense. What a team can do is limited by the skill of its players.

2. If you can't pass and receive the ball, you can't play soccer.

3. If you can't dribble the ball, you won't be successful. Good dribblers give up the ball before they are in trouble, not after they are in trouble.

4. Do not just kick the ball unless it is in a dangerous position in front of our goal.

5. When our team has the ball, everyone is on offense. When the other team has the ball, everyone is on defense.

6. Don't run forward when we have the ball unless you run backward when they have the ball.

7. If you lose the ball, you should be the first person on defense. When changing from offense to defense, sprint to be between your man and our goal.

8. We will work hard to always beat our opponent to the ball. (You have to be in shape!)

9. To be the best player you can be, you have to be able to play and you have to be able to play *smart:*

    A. Say nothing to the referee! He or she is human, too, and will make mistakes.

    B. Never criticize a teammate, especially a goalie after a goal. Before the ball got by him, it got past ten other players.

    C. To play up to your ability, you have to take care of your body.

    D. One hundred percent effort is expected at all times. We might be outplayed, but we won't be out hustled. "I can't" and "I won't" aren't acceptable.

    E. Potential means you haven't done anything yet. The world is full of potentially good players. We want to *reach* our potential.

    F. Win, lose, or draw—we have nothing to be ashamed of as long as we have given 100 percent to the effort.

10. Your job as a player is to HAVE FUN, LEARN, AND SUCCEED, in that order.

As an adult, your job is to make sure that at the end of the season that the children have done all three.

5

THE RULES OF THE GAME AND DIMENSIONS OF THE FIELD

We can hear you now: "What kind of sports instruction book puts rules of the game in the middle of the book? It belongs at the end." Nope, not for soccer. We know that sports books traditionally put the rules at the end, but we think they belong here, early on, because in many cases, assigned coaches *don't know them.* Additionally, lots of good, pertinent advice and instruction may be found right within these rules.

We are introducing the rules from the United States Soccer Federation because we think they best describe the game itself in an easy-to-understand fashion. But be aware that most youth leagues *adapt* the rules of soccer to accommodate the size of the players or the size of their fields. *Make sure you know the rules of your league before you start.* It's not productive to warn or drill your players on the penalty for a bad throw-in being loss of possession, only to find that your league allows another try. Read the rules and your own league's rules carefully.

There are seventeen laws, or rules, of soccer as laid down by the ruling body of soccer, FIFA. These provide guidelines for playing the game. The laws are simple and flexible, yet specific. It is the responsibility of the coach to know and understand these laws thoroughly and to pass this knowledge on to players. In addition to maintaining the spirit of the laws, the coach must be concerned with their tactical application. He can use them to his team's advantage, while staying within their limits.

LAW 1. THE FIELD OF PLAY

The soccer field is rectangular, its length no more than 130 yards nor less than 100 yards and its width not more than 100 yards nor less than 50 yards. At each end are a goal, a goal area, and a penalty area with a penalty spot. In addition, the field is marked with a center circle, center spot, penalty arcs, corner areas, and a halfway line. Flags are placed at each corner of the field and, optionally, at each end of the halfway line.

LAW 2. THE BALL

The ball is spherical and made of leather or other approved material. Its circumference is between 27 and 28 inches and the weight, at the start of the game, between 14 and 16 ounces and inflated to a pressure equal to 0.6 to 1.1 atmospheres (600 to 1,100 g/cm^2) at sea level (8.5 lbs/in^2 to 15.6 lbs/in^2).

The ball cannot be changed without the referee's permission. If the ball bursts or becomes defective during the course of a match, the match is stopped and is restarted by dropping the replacement ball at the place where the first ball became defective. If the ball bursts or becomes defective while not in play at a kickoff, goal kick, corner kick, free kick, penalty kick, or throw-in, the match is restarted accordingly.

LAW 3. THE NUMBER OF PLAYERS

A match is played by two teams, each consisting of not more than eleven players, one of whom is the goalkeeper. A match may not start if either team consists of fewer than seven players. Up to three substitutes may be used in any match played in an official competition under the auspices of FIFA. In national A team matches, up to a maximum of six substitutes may be used. In all other matches, a greater number of substitutes may be used, provided that the teams concerned reach agreement on a maximum number and the referee is informed before the match. If the referee is not informed or no agreement is reached before the match, no more than six substitutes are allowed.

LAW 4. PLAYERS' EQUIPMENT

- The basic compulsory equipment of a player shall consist of a jersey or shirt, shorts, stockings, shin guards, and footwear.
- A player shall not wear anything which is dangerous to another player.
- Shin guards, which must be covered entirely by the stockings, shall be made of a suitable material (rubber, plastic, polyurethane, or similar substance) and shall afford a reasonable degree of protection.
- The goalkeeper shall wear colors which distinguish him from the other players and from the referee.

Punishment:

For any infringement of this law, the player at fault shall be instructed to leave the field of play by the referee, to adjust his equipment or obtain any missing equipment, when the ball next ceases to be in play, unless by then the player has already corrected his equipment. Play shall not be stopped immediately for an infrigement of this law. A player who is instructed to leave the field to adjust his equipment or obtain missing equipment shall not return without first reporting to the referee, who shall satisfy himself that the player's equipment is in order. The player shall only reenter the game at a moment when the ball has ceased to be in play.

LAW 5. THE REFEREE

Each match is controlled by a referee who has full authority to enforce the Laws of the Game in connection with the match to which he has been appointed. The referee's powers and duties are as follows:

- To enforce the Laws of the Game
- To control the match in cooperation with the assistant referees and, where applicable, with the fourth official
- To ensure that any ball used meets the requirements of Law 2
- To act as timekeeper and keep a record of the match
- To stop, suspend, or terminate the match, at his discretion, for any infringements of the Laws
- To stop, suspend, or terminate the match because of outside interference of any kind
- To stop the match if, in his opinion, a player is seriously injured and ensure that he is removed from play. An injured player may return to the field of play only after the match is restarted
- To allow play to continue until the ball is out of play if a player is, in his opinion, only slightly injured

LAW 6. THE ASSISTANT REFEREES

Two assistant referees are appointed whose duties, subject to the referee, are to indicate:

- When the whole of the ball has passed out of play
- Which side is entitled to a corner kick, goal kick, or throw-in
- When a player may be penalized for being in an offside position
- When a substitution is requested
- When misconduct or any other incident has occurred out of view of the referee
- When offenses have been committed whenever the assistants are closer to the action than the referees (this includes, in particular circumstances, offenses committed in the penalty area)
- Whether, at penalty kicks, the goalkeeper has moved forward before the ball has been kicked and if the ball has crossed the line

The assistant referees also assist the referee in controlling the match in accordance with the Laws of the Game. In particular, they may enter the field of play to help control the 9.15 meter distance. In the event of undue interference or improper conduct, the referee will relieve an assistant referee of his duties and make a report to the appropriate authorities.

LAW 7. DURATION OF THE GAME

The duration of the game shall be two equal periods of 45 minutes, unless otherwise mutually agreed upon, subject to the following:

- Allowance shall be made in either period for all time lost through substitution, the transport from the field of injured players, time wasting, or other cause, the amount of which shall be a matter for the discretion of the referee.
- Time shall be extended to permit a penalty kick being taken at or after the expiration of the normal period in either half.
- At halftime the interval shall not exceed fifteen minutes except by consent of the referee.

LAW 8. THE START AND RESTART OF PLAY

A coin is tossed and the team that wins the toss decides which goal it will attack in the first half of the match. The other team takes the kickoff to start the match. The team that wins the toss takes the kickoff to start the second half of the match. In the second half of the match, the teams change ends and attack the opposite goals.

A kickoff is a way of starting or restarting play. Kickoffs are used at the start of the match, after a goal has been scored, at the start of the second half of the match, and at the start of each period of extra time, where applicable. A goal may be scored directly from the kickoff.

LAW 9. BALL IN AND OUT OF PLAY

The ball is out of play when it has wholly crossed the goal line or touch line, whether on the ground or in the air, and play has been stopped by the referee. The ball is in play at all other times, including when it rebounds from a goalpost, crossbar, or corner flag post and remains in the field of play, or if it rebounds from either the referee or an assistant referee when they are on the field of play.

LAW 10. THE METHOD OF SCORING

A goal is scored when the whole of the ball passes over the goal line, between the goalposts and under the crossbar, provided that no infringement of the Laws of the Game has been committed previously by the team scoring the goal. The team scoring the greater number of goals during a match is the winner. If both teams score an equal number of goals, or if no goals are scored, the match is drawn. When competition rules require there to be a winning team after a match or home-and-away tie has been drawn, only the following procedures, which have been approved by the International F.A. Board, are permitted: away goals rule, extra time, and kicks from the penalty mark.

LAW 11. OFFSIDE

It is not an offense in itself to be in an offside position. A player is in an offside position if he is nearer to his opponents' goal line than both the ball and the second last opponent. A player is not in an offside position if he is in his own half of the field of play or he is level with the second last opponent or he is level with the last two opponents.

A player in an offside position is only penalized if, at the moment the ball touches or is played by one of his team, he is, in the opinion of the referee, involved in active play by interfering with play, interfering with an opponent, or gaining an advantage by being in that position.

LAW 12. FOULS AND MISCONDUCT

Fouls and misconduct as penalized as follows:

A direct free kick is awarded to the opposing team if a player commits any of the following six offenses in a manner considered by the referee to be careless, reckless, or using excessive force:

- kicks or attempts to kick an opponent
- trips or attempts to trip an opponent
- jumps at an opponent
- charges an opponent
- strikes or attempts to strike an opponent
- pushes an opponent

A direct free kick is also awarded to the opposing team if a player commits any of the following four offenses:

- tackles an opponent to gain possession of the ball, making contact with the opponent before touching the ball
- holds an opponent
- spits at an opponent
- handles the ball deliberately (except for the goalkeeper within his own penalty area)

A direct free kick is taken from where the offense occurred.

A penalty kick is awarded if any of the above ten offenses is committed by a player inside his own penalty area, irrespective of the position of the ball, provided it is in play.

An indirect free kick is awarded to the opposing team if a goalkeeper, inside his own penalty area, commits any of the following four offenses:

- takes more than six seconds while controlling the ball with his hands before releasing it from his possession
- touches the ball again with his hands after it has been released from his possession and has not touched any other player
- touches the ball with his hands after it has been deliberately kicked to him by a teammate
- touches the ball with his hands after he has received it directly from a throw-in taken by a teammate

An indirect free kick is also awarded to the opposing team if a player, in the opinion of the referee:

- plays in a dangerous manner
- impedes the progress of an opponent
- prevents the goalkeeper from releasing the ball from his hands
- commits any other offense for which play is stopped to caution or dismiss a player

The indirect free kick is taken from where the offense occurred.

CAUTIONABLE OFFENSES—YELLOW CARD

A player is cautioned and shown the yellow card if he commits any of the following seven offenses:

1. is guilty of unsporting behavior
2. shows dissent by word or action
3. persistently infringes the Laws of the Game
4. delays the restart of play
5. fails to respect the required distance when play is restarted with a corner kick, free kick, or throw-in
6. enters or re-enters the field of play without the referee's permission
7. deliberately leaves the field of play without the referee's permission

A substitute or substituted player is cautioned and shown the yellow card if he commits any of the following three offenses:

1. is guilty of unsporting behavior
2. shows dissent by word or action
3. delays the restart of play

SENDING-OFF OFFENSES—RED CARD

A player, substitute, or substituted player is sent off and shown the red card if he commits any of the following seven offenses:

1. is guilty of serious foul play
2. is guilty of violent conduct
3. spits at an opponent or any other person
4. denies the opposing team a goal or an obvious goal-scoring opportunity by deliberately handling the ball (this does not apply to a goalkeeper within his own penalty area)
5. denies an obvious goal-scoring opportunity to an opponent moving toward the player's goal by an offense punishable by a free kick or a penalty kick
6. uses offensive or insulting or abusive language and/or gestures
7. receives a second caution in the same match

A player, substitute, or substituted player who has been sent off and shown the red card must leave the vicinity of the field of play and the technical area.

LAW 13. FREE KICKS

There are two types of free kicks: *direct* (from which a goal can be scored) and *indirect* (from which a goal cannot be scored unless the ball has been played or touched by a player other than the kicker before it passes through the goal). For both direct and indirect free kicks, the ball must be stationary when the kick is taken, and the kicker does not touch the ball a second time until it has touched another player. When a player is taking a free kick outside his own penalty area, all opposing players must remain outside the area and at least 10 yards from the ball. When he is taking a free kick outside his own penalty area, all opposing players must be at least 10 yards from the ball unless they are standing on their own goal line between the goal posts. On free kicks the ball is in play once it is kicked and has moved, and the ball cannot be played again by the kicker until it has been touched by another player.

The referee indicates an indirect free kick by raising his arm above his head. He maintains his arm in that position until the kick has been taken and the ball has touched another player or goes out of play.

LAW 14. THE PENALTY KICK

A penalty kick is awarded against a team that commits one of the ten offenses for which a direct free kick is awarded, inside its own penalty area and while the ball is in play. A goal may be scored directly from a penalty kick. Additional time is allowed for a penalty kick to be taken at the end of each half or at the end of periods of extra time.

The ball is placed on the penalty mark, and the player taking the penalty kick is properly identified. The defending goalkeeper remains on his goal line, facing the kicker, between the goalposts, until the ball has been kicked.

LAW 15. THE THROW-IN

A throw-in is a method of restarting play. The ball is thrown in from the point where it crossed the line by a player of the team opposing that of the person who last touched the ball. A goal cannot be scored directly from a throw-in.

At the moment of delivering the ball, the thrower faces the field of play with part of each foot either on the touch line or on the ground outside the touch line, uses both hands, and delivers the ball from behind and over his head. The thrower may not touch the ball again until it has touched another player.

LAW 16. THE GOAL KICK

A goal kick is awarded when the whole of the ball, having last touched a player of the attacking team, passes over the goal line, either on the ground or in the air, and a goal is not scored in accordance with Law 10.

The ball is kicked from any point within the goal area by a player of the defending team. Opponents remain outside the penalty area until the ball is in play. The kicker does not play the ball a second time until it has touched another player. The ball is in play when it is kicked directly beyond the penalty area. A goal may be scored directly from a goal kick, but only against the opposing team. If the ball is not kicked directly into play beyond the penalty area, the kick is retaken.

LAW 17. THE CORNER KICK

A corner kick is awarded when the whole of the ball, having last touched a player of the defending team, passes over the goal line, either on the ground or in the air, and a goal is not scored in accordance with Law 10. A goal may be scored directly from a corner kick, but only against the opposing team.

The ball is placed inside the corner arc at the nearest corner flag post. The corner flag post is not moved. Opponents remain at least 10 yards from the corner arc until the ball is in play. The ball is kicked by a player of the attacking team, and is in play when it is kicked and moves. The kicker does not play the ball a second time until it has touched another player.

FIELD DIMENSIONS AND TERMINOLOGY

As already mentioned, you must be sure of the specific rules of your league. You must also carefully check the size of the playing field. It really does make a difference when youngsters practice on one size field, only to play their games on a field of another size. Many leagues *have* to adapt their fields, because they're just smaller.

The field in the following diagram is regulation size. We suggest that you diagram your own field so that when you work on your practice plans you can be sure you have enough room and that your drills are run on the same size field as the one you play your games on. (See diagram on next page.)

The old rope trick. In most cases, your practices will be conducted on fields without lines or corners, and sometimes even without goals. But your practice dimensions *must* match game field dimensions. It does no good to work on penalty kicks if, because your field has no penalty spot, you merely guess and end up kicking from 10 yards.

How do you make sure your cones for goals are exactly eight yards apart? Take a piece of string or rope at least as long as the width of your field (regulation 50 yards) and *tie knots at the distances you will need for your field*—for example, 6 yards, 8 yards, 10 yards, 12 yards, 18 yards. This way, when you decide to run a drill from 10 yards out, *you know exactly how far 10 yards is!* This simple trick is a helpful tool for coaches and coaching.

FIELD DIMENSIONS & TERMINOLOGY

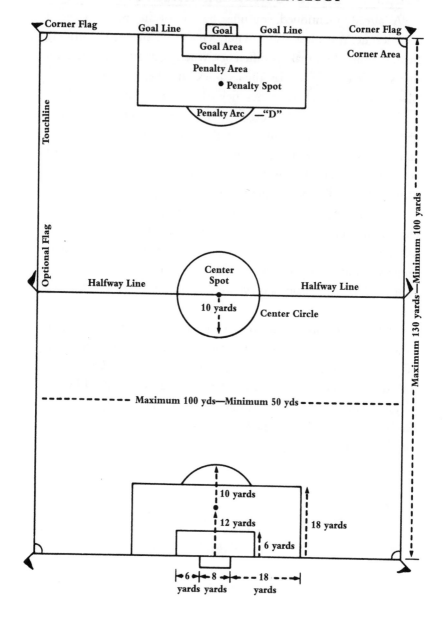

6

JUGGLING

The jugglers you see in the circus keep balls, hoops, clubs, and other objects in the air using mainly their hands and arms. In soccer, however, the player keeps the ball in the air using all parts of his body *except* his arms and hands.

Aside from helping a player become more familiar with the ball, juggling may be the best way to improve a soccer player's balance in a short period of time. It's also fun!

Be certain to emphasize to your players that they are not just juggling to put on a show. It's intended to improve their touch and balance, timing, and foot-eye, thigh-eye, and forehead-eye coordination.

Juggling with the *foot* forces players to use the same concentration they would when shooting the ball. Juggling with the *thigh* forces them to concentrate as they would when receiving an air ball with the thigh. Juggling with the *head* uses the same forehead-eye coordination a player uses when heading a ball for a shot or pass. Juggling, then, is a purposeful skill that will improve touch, balance, and eye coordination with the ball.

Start off by giving each player a ball; if that isn't possible, have partners share a ball. We suggest each player bring his or her own ball to every practice. Tell them to write their names on the balls so they know which is theirs at the end of practice. Be certain that players are spread out to avoid collison. With younger kids you'll want to *really* spread out to prevent the drill from turning into a fire drill.

1. **Thigh.** Have the player toss the ball into the air and, as the ball comes down, bring his thigh up and hit the ball into the air again; the player should catch the ball with his hands and bring the juggling leg back down to the ground.

Remind your players that the thigh should be parallel to the ground or the ball will bounce forward or into the player's body; that they should hit the ball with the center of their thighs; and that the juggling leg should return to the ground after each juggle.

After the ball has been juggled once and caught, the player should try to juggle two consecutive times and catch it. If she is successful with two, let her try to juggle three times. Once the players are able to juggle three times in a row, turn them loose and see how many times they can juggle before missing.

2. **The instep** (the part of the foot where the shoelaces are). Using the same progression as with the thigh, have the players toss and juggle the ball once, twice, and three times before turning them loose. When juggling with the instep, the toe must be pointed and the ankle locked; this simulates the position of the foot when shooting. The laces should be parallel to the ground when contact is made, and the ball should not have any spin on it.

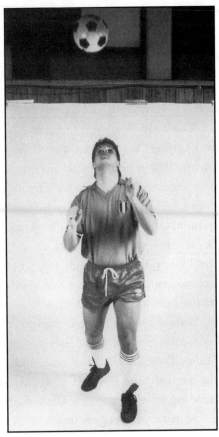

3. **Head:** Follow the same juggling procedure as established above. Instruct the players to hit the ball on their foreheads with their eyes open. They hit the ball; the ball doesn't hit them. Have them lean their heads back to get the back of the head parallel to the ground. They will have to bend their knees a bit as well. The heading force will come from the neck, back, and legs as they juggle.

JUGGLING GAMES

Once the basic juggling techniques have been taught, all sorts of *challenges* are possible. Players can start juggling with the thigh and save the ball with their foot before it hits the ground; players can start with their heads and save only with their feet; or they can alternate body parts by juggling with the head, thigh, and foot, in sequence. The team can have fun seeing which player can juggle the ball farthest across the field, total distance determined by where she last touched the ball. (This precludes just kicking the ball across the field.) Another contest is to see how many times a player can turn in a circle while juggling. Be creative!

PARTNER JUGGLING

There are a number of partner juggling exercises as well. Have two partners stand about 4 or 5 yards away from each other. One partner begins juggling and after three to five juggles passes the ball over to her partner. Then the partner juggles three to five times and passes the ball back. This exercise can also involve three players. Keep in mind our philosophy of not asking kids to do things they can't do. Some youngsters find it difficult to juggle, so don't force them. Instead, allow players to juggle after a bounce. This will give them more time to get ready for each touch. For younger players, if this proves to be too difficult, bring out some beach balls or balloons for the activity. Besides helping them to improve, it can be lots of fun.

Goalkeepers can also have fun juggling using all parts of their bodies. They can challenge one another by punching a soccer ball in the air with one hand, or with two hands together. They can also hand juggle while running across the field or with a partner.

So have your players juggle in practice and encourage them to practice at home on their own. The only investment your players make is their time, which is a small price to pay, considering the improvement they will exhibit in touch-the-ball and body coordination. Mastering this small skill will have a dramatic impact on your players' ability to control the ball.

7 THE SKILLS OF SOCCER

There are some skills that *all* soccer players must have to be successful. Without them, the game is reduced to someone kicking the ball down the field and someone else running after it. Unfortunately, many games are played in this manner, and "kickball" would more realistically describe what is taking place. It is up to the coaches to demand that youngsters not just kick the ball but, rather, exhibit the ability to *control the ball* and then do something constructive with it. The player must feel that the ball is a part of him and not an alien being trying to trip him up. Only through *perfect* repetition of the skills can a skillful player emerge.

SHOOTING

If there is one weakness Americans display most in international soccer, it is the inability to put the ball into the net. We believe kids don't spend enough time actually shooting the ball the way they would in a game. A coach may simply place a ball down on the ground in front of the goal and have the players run up and kick it.

35

We're not helping our youngsters become proficient shooters or scorers with this type of practice.

While this type of fundamental exercise with a still ball is important for younger players, they will have to progress to shooting moving balls, balls that come at them from different angles, balls that are on the ground, and balls that come to them in the air. Let's look at some of the basic elements and rules of shooting:

1. **Regardless of where you strike the ball, your ankle must be locked.** Remind your players to keep their heads and toes down. In keeping their heads down, they will concentrate on striking the center of the ball; keeping their toes down will present the proper surface to the ball.

2. **It doesn't matter how hard you swing your leg; if you hit only part of the ball, it won't go far and it won't go straight.** Players must strike the center of the ball if they want to drive the ball hard.

3. **When striking the ball, your players must have the knee of the kicking foot even with the ball.** If the knee is behind the ball when kicked, it will cause the player to have to reach for it, and thus strike it below the midline—causing the ball to fly up.

4. **The nonkicking foot must step in the direction you want the shot to go and should be next to the ball.** If you watch carefully, you will see that your players' accuracy will be in direct correlation to this simple rule.

5. **The size of the feet can create difficulty when trying to get players to kick the ball with their insteps.** Hate to say it, Coach, but some kids have bigger feet than others, and the bigger-footed kids will have some problems kicking with their insteps.

Let's examine this foot problem a little more closely: players with bigger feet have difficulty because they are sometimes afraid of stubbing their toes on the ground and so will raise their legs a bit and only strike the ball with the *bottom third of the foot*.

Big-footed players also tend to bring their toes up and curl their

feet around the ball as they kick. This generates little power because the ankles unlock.

How to help the big-footed player strike the ball with the instep: (Get a bigger ball! No, only kidding . . .)

Players with bigger feet should approach the ball from a 45-degree angle and step farther away from the ball. Then, by turning their big toes outward and striking the ball with the inside eyelets of their shoes, they will gain the same result.

You can also direct big-footed players to strike the ball with the toes DOWN and inward, using the outside eyelets of the shoe.

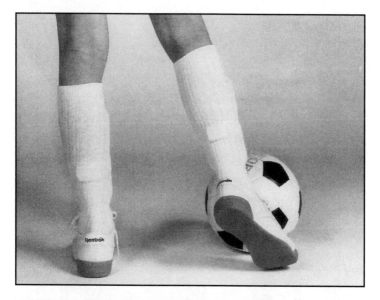

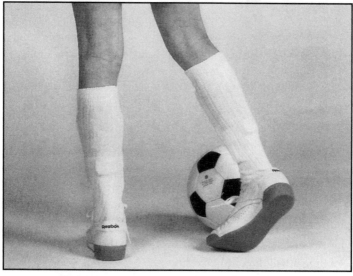

We can't overemphasize the importance of developing *power* in our shots and passes by developing the skill to strike the ball with the instep of the foot. WORK ON IT, COACH, AND YOU'LL SEE THE DIFFERENCE QUICKLY.

BENDING THE BALL

Now that we have explained how to kick the ball straight and strong, let's take a look at the bending ball.

Bending a ball results when the ball is struck by your players *across the ball,* rather than straight on. Needless to say, in order to make it curve, it must be in the air, and as a result we teach our players to strike the ball *below the midline of the ball.* If you do that, you will "bend it like Beckham"!

When trying to shoot the ball around defenders, a defensive wall, or the goalie's outstretched hands, bending the ball is a great tactic.

Remember, the ball is struck with the inside of the shoe above the big toe and the inside eyelets, across the ball and under its midline.

HEADING

We use our feet to propel the ball, and our thighs or feet to stop the ball, but the toughest trick for your players is using the head to either propel the ball or gather it. Kids just aren't used to hitting their heads against moving objects. But anyone who knows soccer realizes that heading is one of the most important skills in the game. Let's look at the progression for teaching heading:

1. Your players' attitude must be that *they are going to hit the ball, rather than let the ball hit them.*

2. Your players must be taught that the proper place to make contact with the ball in a header is with the forehead, not the top of the head.

3. The only way your players can ensure making contact with the forehead is for them to *keep their eyes open,* the most important skill for heading.

4. Your players should clench their teeth, which tightens their neck muscles and so firms the position of the head; this results in a more powerful header. (It also prevents biting the tongue.)

5. To increase power, your players should *arch their backs.*

6. A sharp bending forward after contact also results in increased power, so your players must understand that heading is learned from the *waist up.*

> **REMINDER:** STRIKE THE BALL WITH THE CENTER OF THE FOREHEAD. KEEP THE EYES OPEN. HIT THE BALL—DON'T LET THE BALL HIT YOU.

Some leagues allow foam or safety head gear. In some modified leagues goalkeepers are mandated to wear the head gear and a mouthguard. If this helps your players to succeed, use them.

PASSING

There's a saying in soccer that if you can't pass, you can't play soccer. That statement is true. There is nothing more frustrating to a soccer team than having a player standing in front of the goal, wide open, ready to score a winning goal, only to have the pass be long, short, or wide.

> **THE RULES:** YOUR PLAYERS MUST BE ABLE TO PASS THE BALL TO A TEAMMATE, OR TO A SPACE—AND WITH PROPER PACE.

Let's see what this means:

PASSING TO A TEAMMATE

You might think this is a pretty obvious concept; when your teammate is open, you can pass to him. But it's not as simple as you think. When the player with the ball gets his head up and sees a teammate that he can pass to, he now knows where his teammate is located. But does he know where the closest defender is located? If the defender is directly behind his team-mate and slightly to one side, the pass must be played to the foot on the opposite side of the defender. Passing directly at your team-mate may allow the defender to run around him and intercept the ball.

PASSING TO A SPACE

The game of soccer is a game of space—space between people, space between the goalie and the goalposts, space between defender and attacker. Your passing players must often be looking to pass the ball into an AREA rather than directly to a man. This is passing into space. (The corresponding skill for the receiver is RUNNING INTO SPACE.) Remember, the receiver knows what space she is going to run into; the defender doesn't. This is one of the advantages to having possession of the ball: your passer must understand space, practice passing into it, and realize how important it is.

PASSING WITH PROPER PACE . . .

Proper pace means that the ball is passed in such a way that the receiver may ONE-TOUCH the ball, not control it and pass it with a second touch. But a ball that is passed too softly (hospital ball) could hurt your teammate (collision may result because the defender can get there just as quickly as your teammate) and usually will result in loss of possession, too. A ball struck too hard (the bullet) usually results in the teammate not being able to gather the ball. Needless to say, one-touching the bullet is almost an impossibility. TWO TOUCHES, which means just what it says—touching the ball twice (control, kick)—is frankly how most players play a pass. Of course, it must be practiced. We'll deal with receiving later on.

A very important result of passing the ball with the proper pace is that it allows the receiver to take a "second look." Here's what we mean: as a receiver runs into a space to receive a pass, he reads the direction of the ball. As he is running toward the spot where he will actually first touch the ball, he has an opportunity to get his head up and take a "second look." He is looking to find other teammates (in case he has to one-touch the ball to them), the goal (in the event he

can take a one-time shot), and defenders (in the event he has to redirect the ball as he receives it and quickly move away from the defender). The only way a player can take a "second look" is if the ball is passed at the proper pace, so you really have to stress this point at all of your practices.

OTHER PASSING RULES

1. The foot doesn't lie. Whatever direction the foot is facing is the direction the ball will go.

2. Receivers can do more harm than good by yelling for the ball.

How often do you hear players yell for the ball and have it passed to them, only to see it lost? The fact is that if the offensive player hears the yell, so does the defensive player. Your players must pass ONLY WHEN THEY ARE READY.

PASSING SKILLS

Now let's look at the different types of passes and how to teach them.

Push pass—The most frequently used pass in the game today is the push pass, or inside-of-the-foot pass. The rules for teaching and practicing this pass are:

1. The ankle must be locked.

2. The kicking foot is turned sideways to the ball.

3. The ball is struck below the ankle bone and closer to the middle of the foot.

4. The ball is struck as close to the midline as possible.

5. After striking the ball, the player should raise his knee up, which will give the ball topspin, resulting in the ball moving more quickly.

6. The lower leg should swing through like a pendulum.

7. The nonkicking foot is pointed . . . where? That's right, in the direction the player wants the ball to go.

If you ask your players to FREEZE after kicking the ball, you will be able to see if their technique is correct or not. If correct, the inside of the foot will be facing the receiver.

Outside-of-the-foot pass—The outside of the foot is often used for passing, and the rules for using it are somewhat more difficult to teach, but nevertheless important:

1. When kicking the ball with the outside of the foot, the AN-KLE MUST BE LOCKED. (Have you heard this enough?)
2. The player should point her toe DOWN, and inward.
3. The nonkicking foot should be turned slightly AWAY FROM THE BALL. That's different, eh? By stepping away, it will give the player a bit more room for the kicking foot to come through.

4. The heel of the kicking foot, when brought back to strike the ball, should be brought back BEHIND THE KNEE OF THE NON-KICKING FOOT.

5. Of course, we have our players strike the center of the ball, but this time just above the baby toe.

Chip pass—When the ball is lofted with backspin, it's called a chip. Here are the steps in teaching it:

1. The ball is struck with the INSIDE EYELETS of the shoe.

2. When bringing the kicking foot back, bring it back to the BACKSIDE.

3. The knee must SNAP when coming forward. Again, the best way to see if the technique is correct is to FREEZE the player after contact. Remember, the backspin will result only if the ball is struck below the midline with a LOCKED ANKLE.

RECEIVING

Now that you've taught your kids how to pass and head the ball, let's deal with the guy on the other end—the RECEIVER.

In the past, receiving has been called trapping, though it doesn't matter what it is called. The skill demands mastering the art of gathering in the ball in order to do something else with it. Stress that RECEIVING ALWAYS LEADS TO SOMETHING ELSE; in that way your players are motivated to learn and work on this important skill. Simply put, when receiving the ball, the player will redirect the ball and dribble, pass, or take a shot.

Here's how to teach receiving:

1. Players must be able to receive the ball with every legal body part—foot, thigh, head, chest, etc.

2. Players must "read" the flight or run of the ball so that they can center the body on the ball.

3. Once the ball flight or run is read, the player can decide which body part will receive the ball.

4. Next, your player is to PRESENT that body part to the ball.

5. As the ball makes contact, the body part must be DRAWN BACK slightly for the "give" that results in control.

6. A short HOP just before contact will help your players stay on their toes and off their heels, thus cushioning the blow and helping with control.

RECEIVING WITH DIFFERENT BODY PARTS

Sole of the foot—It's easiest to teach players to receive with the bottom of the foot. Have players lift their toes off the ground slightly as the ball is kicked their way and cushion the ball as it makes contact.

Have your players pretend the ball is an egg, and they will understand how lightly it must be touched.

Side of the foot (ball in the air)—As the ball comes toward the player, he should angle the lower leg from the knee down to the foot. Then, using the inside of the foot and angling the leg over the ball, redirect it to the side of the foot and gather it.

This technique can be accomplished with either the inside or the outside of the ankle.

Side of the foot (ball on the ground)—As the ball comes toward the player, he should bring the toe up and angle the foot to the side. Contact the ball with the side of the foot and redirect it across your body and away from a defender.

Bottom third of the foot or lower instep—This method is usually used for air balls. Have your players relax their ankle to cushion the ball.

Then, by giving way a little, the player can literally catch the ball on top of the bottom third of the foot.

Thigh—The thigh is larger and softer than the other parts of the body, but the rules are the same: read the flight of the ball; present the surface (thigh); take a slight hop before contact; bring the leg down upon contact. Again, this obviously works only for air balls.

Chest—For the chest "trap" it is important that you teach your players to make contact with HALF of the chest, rather than straight on. This is because with the sternum, or chest bone, right in the middle, balls taken straight on can bounce away. (A football receiver who has a perfectly thrown pass bounce off his chest because he let it go through his hands directly onto his shoulder pads illustrates the same

principle.) Using half of the chest will result in contact with the fleshy part and provide more control. The ball can also be redirected easier. The rules for receiving with the chest, however, are the same as with other body parts.

Head—This may come as a surprise, but the head can also be used to receive the ball. How? Teach your players to "give" with the neck and back at contact and try to contact the ball as it is coming down. Obviously this means they will jump in the air to receive with the head.

Needless to say, your players should be taught to receive the ball with the foot whenever possible because any other reception requires TWO TOUCHES to control the ball and do something else with it.

DRIBBLING

Simply defined, dribbling consists of tiny touches of the ball, usually in close quarters. When dribbling, as in the performance of other skills of the game, players must be able to use all parts of the foot—the inside, outside, top, and sole. Your players must be able to change speed, change direction, and dribble with their heads up. (There are only two times when soccer players should have their heads down: when the player first touches the ball, and when it is last touched.) Keeping the head up is essential because otherwise your players will not be able to see their teammates, defenders, or the goal.

Changing speed—Successful control of the ball while dribbling means that your players must be able to alter their pace of dribbling. A defending player has a much better chance of taking the ball away if the dribbler continues at an even pace. Teach your players to vary their speed and they will have much more success keeping the ball.

Changing direction—If your players can change speed, but only in a straight line, they aren't going to be very difficult to stop. Players must be able to move the ball back and forth and change position while dribbling. Starting right and going left; starting left and going right; even starting forward and sometimes moving back are direction changes that must be taught and practiced.

Head up—Just to reiterate, your players can't play if they can't see. The head-up principle must be stressed and restressed. If you can't *see*, you can't be successful in soccer.

One foot versus two feet—Many soccer coaches emphasize that a player must be able to play with both feet. This is certainly true, but coaches often overemphasize this skill.

When talking about and teaching dribbling, few players are equally proficient with both feet. Most of them have a dominant foot and an efficient foot. (Franz Beckenbauer, an outstanding German player who played with the Cosmos in the United States, played few balls with his left foot because his right foot was so dominant he could do anything with it. By using both the inside and outside of his right foot, he became one of the greatest passers in soccer history.)

The fact is, players can attack much more quickly while dribbling with only one foot.

When players hold on to the ball too long—As players learn to dribble better, they gain confidence and can sometimes get into the bad habit of holding on to the ball too long. This is not unusual. Certainly, there are times when you *want* the player to keep the ball and attack the defense, e.g., the player may have a 1v1 opportunity close to the goal and a great chance to score. While we don't want to take away the creativity and desire of a player to beat a defender, in certain situations passing the ball is more productive. For example, player A has the ball at midfield, beats a defender, and continues to dribble down the field. While it's great that he beat the defender, the defender won't be beaten for very long. The defender will recover quickly, chase the player with the ball, and eventually catch up to him since he doesn't have a ball to slow him down.

When a defender is beaten, usually another defender will move toward the attacker with the ball and leave the person they were defending open. Now is the time to pass the ball ahead to the unmarked teammate, who has moved into an open space to receive the pass. After the ball is passed, the passer must keep running. His job has just begun. The player might get the ball right back and still be on the attack.

A great time to point out this basic concept of passing instead of dribbling is during practice. As soon as one of your players holds on to the ball in a drill and continues dribbling when a pass should have been made, stop play. Bring the team together and tell them you are going to explain why a pass would have been a better option than dribbling.

Pick out the fastest player on your team and have him stand next to you. Have an assistant coach or another player stand about 20 yards away. With the ball at your feet, tell the fast player you are going to have a race. The finish line is the assistant coach or another player. When you say, "go!" to start the race, pass the ball to the coach or player as the fast player starts to run. Who wins the 20-yard race, the fast player or the ball? Of course, the ball gets there much faster, as no one can outrun the ball!

Another outgrowth of passing the ball to a teammate instead of dribbling is that you have bypassed all of the defenders between the ball and the receiver. If the person with the ball kept dribbling it, he would still have all of those defenders between him and the receiver.

DRIVING

Driving means that instead of working in a small area with many defenders, the player has more room and can literally pass the ball to himself. The best way to describe driving is by example: perhaps your wing is turning at midfield and has beaten the defender. He doesn't want the ball to slow him down. His best bet, then, is to push the ball ahead of him into space so that as he runs toward the ball, he can make a decision as to what to do next. Just how far he pushes it will depend on how much space he has to work with.

SHIELDING

All good dribblers must know shielding. Similar to the basketball technique where the dribbler keeps the ball away from the defender with his body, shielding in soccer means that the dribbler keeps his body between the defender and the ball. But don't allow players to turn their backs on the defender, which invites an easy reach for the ball, either through or around the dribbler's legs. When the dribbler turns his back he will also have trouble beating the defender one on one—he can't see the defender or his teammates.

Proper shielding technique is a sideways turn—which makes the player WIDER and shields the ball more effectively. This also allows your player to lean into the defender and open up his field of vision to better see a teammate or take a shot on goal.

WRONG

RIGHT

8

EXERCISES TO IMPROVE SKILLS (Techniques)

It is the nature of the game that all of the players on the field must be able to perform all of the sport's various skills. Each player, regardless of position, will be called upon to head, pass, receive, shoot, and dribble during the game.

Your job, as a youth league coach, is to teach these skills and drill your players on when and how to use them.

At higher levels of play, players assigned to certain positions for the majority of a game may spend practice time doing *functional* training. This involves backs, midfielders, and strikers (forwards), training to do (technically and tactically) what they will be called upon to do in a game, *most* of the time. As you may have noticed, this book is geared toward an overall development of skill for all players.

Many of the exercises introduced here involve using more than one skill at a time. As a coach you must determine which single skill you are trying to improve upon during an offensive tactic and *comment only on that skill, even if you are inclined to comment on others.* During play, try to determine if this exercise is meeting your goal to improve a specific skill. If it isn't, try to break down the exercise to a more fundamental level.

For example, if shooting is the goal of an exercise, but you do not get very many shots on goal, then you should change the exercise. Replace the defender with a cone (or a coach playing passive defense) and explain that a shot must be taken every time, or that the defender is not allowed to steal the ball. Don't be afraid to change the exercise if you have given it a fair chance to succeed at meeting a particular goal and it hasn't worked. We can't stress enough the importance of being flexible and understanding your young players. If a drill you are using doesn't work, for goodness' sake END IT and move on. A skill practiced incorrectly will result in that skill being done incorrectly at game time.

THINGS TO THINK ABOUT WHEN DESIGNING DRILLS

1. *If you ask a player to do something he can't do, you are wrong; if you ask a player to do something he can do and he doesn't, then he's wrong.* If you decide he can do it and he doesn't, then you, as coach, must try to determine what the problem is. Is it his subtle misunderstanding of what to do? Is he able to perform the skill but only under limited pressure? Can he do what you ask, but only three times out of ten? When you determine the reason he is unsuccessful, then you must develop a program for him to be successful—or accept the fact that at *this time* he is not able to perform that skill.

2. *Youngsters will remember about 50 percent of what they are told, 60 percent of what they see, 75 percent of what they do, and 85 percent of what they teach.* Quite often coaches find themselves pressured with limited practice time and will only *tell* a youngster what to do. Some may show what they want as well. The most successful coaches will give their players sufficient opportunities to try the task, and some may even ask their players to explain what they are doing as a coach would. In this way the player learns, without question, what is expected.

3. *When teaching a technique, it must be done perfectly.* Even the most inexperienced coach can demonstrate a skill efficiently if it is done

in slow motion, step-by-step. Players must see and then practice the technique perfectly. The old adage "practice makes perfect" is wrong. *Practice makes permanent; perfect practice makes perfect.*

4. *When coaching, stay positive and stay clear of using the word "don't."* Instead, instruct your players to *do* something. By using a positive statement, you reinforce your instructions in their mind. (The same can be said for negative statements. If someone were to say to you, "Don't think of a pink elephant," you would immediately think of a pink elephant!) If you want your players to think of certain things on the field, reinforce them positively. "Tommy, pass the ball more" will help Tommy more than "Don't dribble so much, Tommy."

5. *Avoid "waste" drills that take up valuable time.* Use exercises that develop what players will do in a game. Each exercise should have a purpose and help you meet team goals. Remember that when setting up a practice area (grid), the size of the area will depend upon the number of players and their skill levels. Don't be afraid to adjust the size of the grid if you have miscalculated.

6. *Distance rule.* As we said in Rule 1: if you ask a player to do something he can't do, you are wrong. Similarly, if you should ask him to do something he can do, but you make the conditions such that he can't, you're wrong again. For example, if you are working on receiving and your players cannot pass accurately from more than 10 yards away, they will surely fail if they are placed 25 yards apart.

7. *Make your drills fun.* We are not suggesting you always try to laugh and enjoy yourselves as a team when you are learning a new skill and working on it. However, we do believe the more fun you can make a drill, the better chance you have that your kids will pick it up and work on it. Think before you set up a drill. How can you make sure the players enjoy doing it? How can you add a little competition within the drill to get their adrenaline flowing? It isn't hard to do this, Coach, it just takes some work on your part. If your kids think your drills are "games," you've made them fun.

Remember, there is nothing worse in sports than a boring practice!

Here are some exercises to help turn your young ones into America's next Mia Hamms or Landon Donovans. Keep in mind that many of the exercises use a number of skills. Stress only the skills you are trying to improve.

SHOOTING

> **REMEMBER THE RULES:** HEAD DOWN/TOE DOWN/ LOCK THE ANKLE AND DON'T LET IT MOVE; STRIKE THE CENTER OF THE BALL WITH THE LACES.

1. **Tap/tap.** Many youngsters don't know what it feels like to have the ball hit their insteps (laces). So let them kneel on one knee and bang a ball on the laces of their front feet.

With that accomplished, have a coach place his foot just above the midline of the ball, and let each player strike the center of the ball solidly with their laces. Make certain they don't swing too hard and miss, or the coach may need new shins!

2. **Punting.** With that in mind, now let the players get a partner and share one ball. From a 10-yard distance have the players punt the ball back and forth to each other like a football. They should concentrate on striking the ball just before it hits the ground. Explain that the ball is not allowed to travel higher than their waists. Tell them that you want to see how many times in a row they can catch the ball. This exercise will help remove the fear some youngsters have of hitting their toes on the ground as they shoot.

3. **Still balls.** After reviewing the proper technique of shooting the ball, have both partners now shoot still balls on the ground to one another from 10 yards away. Tell the players to pretend that their shot is just a pass (around the goalkeeper) and to strike the ball solidly but not so hard that their partner can't control the ball. At this point, some players may still be afraid of stubbing their toes and make the two most common mistakes: raising their feet at contact and curling their toes up and around the ball (unlocking the ankle).

It may be necessary to go back to a few of the previous exercises to try to correct these problems.

4. **Moving balls.** Have the players back up to about 20 yards and remain with their partners. Now the player with the ball will push the ball forward 2 to 3 yards, run toward it, step, and shoot. Immediately you will find many youngsters shooting balls over the goal height of eight feet. Explain that this happens because, as they step even with the ball to shoot, the ball continues to roll and lies ahead of

their feet when they actually hit it. So they reach for the ball and strike under its middle, sending it flying into the air. The solution is to step *beyond* the ball when kicking a moving ball. How far the player steps beyond the ball depends on how fast it is rolling. Have the player continue to push the balls ahead and strike them. You should see improvement.

5. Slalom and shoot. This exercise offers more of a game-like situation. Set up four cones on each side of where the penalty area meets the penalty arc. (See Field Dimensions Diagram in Chapter 5.)

Have two groups of players line up behind these cones; the cones should be about 2 yards apart. The first person on line dribbles in and out of the cones (slalom) and shoots. As soon as the shooter strikes the ball, the first person in the other line begins. Be certain to stress that players should shoot with both feet and keep the shot low. After a few minutes of shooting, stop the action and remind the players of the importance of keeping the ball low: low shots are harder for a

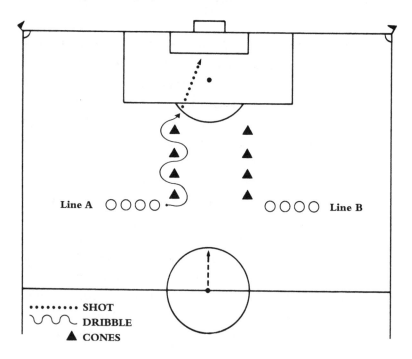

Line A

Line B

·········· SHOT
∿∿∿ DRIBBLE
▲ CONES

young goalkeeper to dive and save; low balls may deflect off a post or body and go in (even if it is a wide shot); low shots may be blocked by the goalkeeper and the rebound kicked in. A goalkeeper may be screened or "blinded" by his teammate on a low kick; a high shot will simply sail over the goal.

6. **Coach's toss.** The next shooting exercise is a more strenuous one-on-one (1v1) confrontation. Form two lines on the corners of the penalty box. The coach stands 25 yards away and says "go!" The first person in each line runs toward the arc (D), and the coach passes the ball between the players, alternating air and ground passes. The players fight to control the ball and have five seconds to get off a shot.

A variation of this drill would be to have two players on each side come out; before a team can shoot, both players must touch the ball.

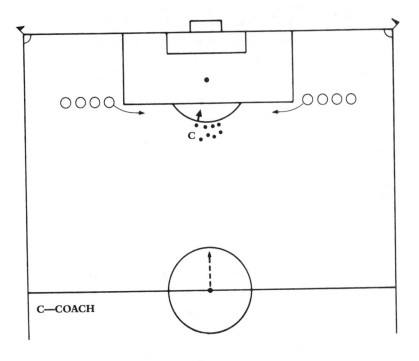

C—COACH

7. **Eight-second shot drill.** Set up a mini-field 35 yards long, at the regular field width. Put a goalie in each goal. Have the goalies put extra balls inside the goal, ready to be put into play. Form teams of

four to six players on a side. The object is for them to score goals *as a team*. There are only two restrictions: the goalie can only roll the ball out, rather than kick or throw it, and as soon as a field player touches the ball, a shot must be taken on the goal within eight seconds. (Be flexible with the time.)

During each of these shooting exercises it is imperative to stress the proper mental approach toward shooting. Players must realize that they have a responsibility and an obligation to shoot when the opportunity presents itself.

A missed opportunity is lost forever. Your players' attitude must be, "If I'm within my shooting range, I must shoot!"

HEADING

REMEMBER THE RULES: EYES OPEN; HIT THE FORE-HEAD; TIGHTEN TEETH; YOU HIT THE BALL, DON'T LET THE BALL HIT YOU.

Heading is one of the more difficult skills to teach youngsters because they tend to fear getting hit on their noses, cheeks, mouths, eyes, tops of their heads, etc. Remind them that in order to head the ball on the part that won't hurt (the forehead), they must keep their eyes open. That is easier said than done, however. To develop your young players' confidence in heading the ball, a wise investment might be a couple of Nerf balls. Then they can miss painlessly as they teach themselves the skill.

1. **Thanks, I needed that.** Have your players pair up and share a ball with their partners. In turn, have each player hold the ball in both hands and hit his forehead ten times. When finished, both players know what it feels like to have their heads hit a ball in the correct place. They also realize that they are still in good shape and ready for another challenge.

2. Head to your partner. The first partner now attempts to hold the ball in both hands and head it out of his hands to his partner 5 yards away. Explain that to get the extra power for heading, it is necessary to arch the back and then snap forward.

3. **Heading the tossed ball.** This next step will build your players' confidence in heading a tossed ball. Young players may have difficulty tossing a soccer ball, so the coach should be ready to toss it for them. The age and skill of the players will determine if you want to use Nerf or regular balls. For ten- or eleven-year-olds you might even think about gently tossing tennis balls underhand. It will help them to concentrate on the ball. They will also realize that anyone who can head a tennis ball can't possibly miss a big soccer ball. Remember not to be farther than 10 yards away when you toss.

4. **Toss and move.** (Note: These exercises require a good toss. You may have to be the tosser.) This exercise continues the tossing-and-heading drill while the players are moving. Partners should stand 2 to 3 yards apart. The tosser runs backward across the field as the header runs forward. The partners toss and head back to each other as they go across the field. When they reach the other side, have the partners switch roles, the tosser running forward and the header run-

ning backward. This drill presumes a high level of skill; only you can
determine if your players are up to it.

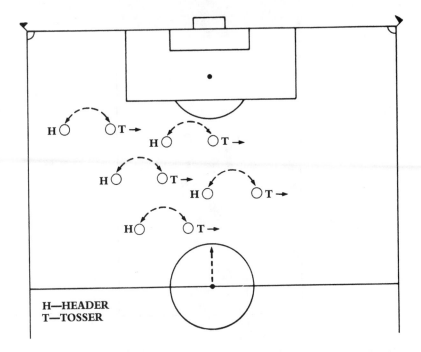

H—HEADER
T—TOSSER

5. **Directing with the head.** The next skill your soccer players
need to develop is the ability to direct the ball with their heads. Make
certain that your players have lots of room. The tosser begins by making an underhand toss to the header. Immediately, the tosser moves
to the right or left. The header must perceive the direction in which
the tosser moves and head it to him.

6. **Individual head juggling.** Each player juggles the ball in the
air using the head only.

Here's a fun idea: have heading contests at practice using the
drills just described and give awards for the leaders when the practice
is finished. Lollipops may be an appropriate reward—sugarless, of
course!

7. **Run-on header.** These exercises are more game-related. The
simplest is to have a coach stand at the side of the goal with the soc-

cer balls. One player acts as goalie while the others line up even with the opposite post, about 18 yards away. The first header runs toward the center of the goal. Toss the ball in the air about 8 yards from the goal. The player times the flight of the ball and tries to head it into the goal.

Then the header becomes the new goalie. The previous goalie chases the ball, sets it down by the coach, and moves to the end of the heading line. For a challenge, place cones approximately 12 yards in front of the goal. The header must now leap over the cones, regain his balance, find the ball, and head it into the goal. The coach must time his toss to give the header a chance to head the ball. Allow more time for less athletic youngsters.

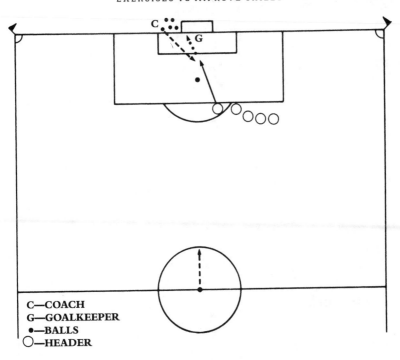

C—COACH
G—GOALKEEPER
●—BALLS
○—HEADER

8. **Lay-back shoot.** The next exercise combines heading and a shot on goal by a second player. The heading player stands with his back to the goal. He is on the penalty spot (12 yards away). The remaining players line up with a ball where the penalty arc (D) and penalty area line meet. The first player in line tosses the ball to the header and moves to the other side of the arc (D). The header lays the ball back to the tosser, who shoots on goal. The shooter now runs to the penalty spot and becomes the new header. The previous header rotates to the end of the line. Remember, the kid hits the ball; the ball doesn't hit the kid!

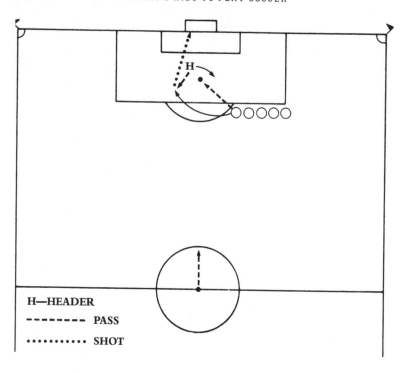

H—HEADER

- - - - - - - - PASS

• • • • • • • • • • • • SHOT

PASSING

REMEMBER THE RULE: PASS TO A PLAYER OR SPACE WITH PROPER PACE.

1. **Wishbone soccer.** Have partners stand 5 yards apart. They stand with their legs as goals about 2 feet apart. Have each partner see how many times in five tries he can pass the ball through the other player's legs.

2. Passing and Redirecting. In this drill, partners can move farther apart if they pass the ball successfully at a closer distance. This will depend upon their ability, age, and strength. Have the players start about 4 yards apart and pass back and forth using the insides of their feet. Players should also receive the ball using only the insides of their feet and should also use only two touches with this drill—receive the ball with one touch and pass it back with the second.

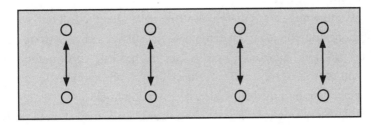

This is a great time for you and your coaches to watch the techniques the players are using. Some players will have difficulty and not be able to pass accurately from this distance. Move them in a bit and have them focus on using good technique. Concentrate on each player's technique. If they cannot pass without pressure from a short distance, they will not be able to pass successfully from greater distances in a game.

Once the players start to have some success, put restrictions on their passing—have them pass only with:

The inside of the right foot
The inside of the left foot
Alternating the inside of the left/right foot

Then have the players alternate receiving the ball with:

The inside of the right foot
The inside of the left foot
Alternating the inside of the left/right foot

Now let's talk about redirecting the ball. Redirecting means that when a player receives a pass, he moves the ball into a space away from where he first touched the ball. This is a very important skill.

When a player is being defended (marked), the defender will anticipate a pass to the offensive player before the pass is even made. As a result, the defender moves to intercept the pass before it is received. If the receiving player stops the ball at her feet, the defender will have a great opportunity to steal the ball, or at least put pressure on the person with the ball.

Redirecting means the offensive player pushes the ball into space without stopping it and gives the defensive player a chance to steal it. This will give him more time to get his head up to find another teammate to pass to, to shoot at the goal, or to just continue to maintain possession of the ball while dribbling downfield.

Now let's practice this skill. Have your players stand about 4 yards apart and pass the ball back and forth. When the ball is passed toward their right foot, they should redirect it with the inside of their right foot across their body to the left side (make sure they have their toes up and angle their foot across their bodies). Then have them pass the ball back with their left feet. This simple drill lets them feel what it is like to move the ball quickly without stopping it and still maintain control.

Each player can alternate trying to pass the ball to the right and left foot so their partners can practice redirecting the ball with both feet and passing it back with both feet as well. Once they get the idea, you can have them redirect and pass the ball with the outsides of their feet as well.

Players must always be on the balls of their feet and have their feet moving. If a player is moving in the wrong direction as he starts to run to the ball, he can still get to the ball faster than if he is standing still.

You should also encourage your players to be "dancing" before they receive the ball. Tell them to stay on the balls of their feet. You can also tell them that they must be running in place at least ten steps after they pass the ball to their partner and are waiting to receive a pass back.

3. **Pass—Defend—Replace.** In this exercise, passing and receiving skills are developed as the players are moving. Three players line up in a straight line across the field. The players start out 8 to 10 yards away from one another. The player in the middle starts with the ball and passes it to a player at one end. After passing the ball, the passer follows her pass and runs toward the receiver, stopping one yard in front of her in a defensive posture. (She does not try to steal the ball.) The receiver makes a 1v1 move and goes by the stationary defender. The original passer/defender then replaces the player who received the pass and stands where she was standing.

Once the receiver has completed her 1v1 move, she passes to the third partner at the other end of the line. After passing to her on the run (like in a game), the new passer follows her pass and becomes a stationary defender one yard in front of the new receiver. The new receiver makes a 1v1 move past the stationary defender. The stationary defender replaces the player making the 1v1 move as that player passes the ball to the partner on the far end again. This pattern continues without stoppage of play from passing to defending to replacing the partner who goes on offense.

Player B passes to C, follows her pass, plays passive defense, and then replaces player C. Player C does a 1v1 move past B, passes to player A, and follows her pass to play passive defense and then replace player A. Player A then passes to player B, and the exercise continues in the same manner until stopped.

Don't worry if you have an odd number of players on your team

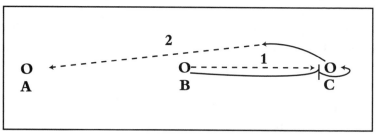

and can't break up into threes. All you have to do is put four players in a group, with two starting at one end and the first player in line going first. When the ball comes back in that direction, the second player will go.

PASS-DEFEND-REPLACE (WITH A WALL PLAYER)

A great variation to this drill is to add a fourth person as a *wall player*. The three players in a straight line continue to move in the same manner as before—Pass-Defend-Replace. Now, however, a wall player is added, who runs from one end to the other. When the pass is made to one end, the wall player runs to that end and gets square with the player with the ball. The receiver receives the ball and instead of doing a 1v1 move passes the ball to the wall player and

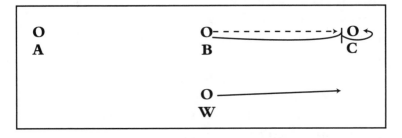

moves around the defender to receive a pass back. (This is called a "Wall Pass," and we will go over this more in a later chapter.)

After receiving the return pass, the player with the ball passes it to the person at the other end of the line. The wall player never stops. She runs to the other end of the line to become the wall for that person. The exercise continues back and forth in both directions. This

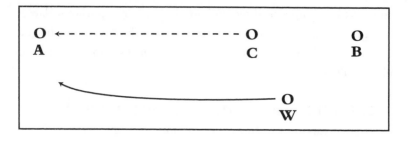

can certainly test the fitness of players and their ability to execute skills at game speed when tired. After a few minutes, switch players around so that everyone can become the neutral player. You may also choose to add a wall on both sides of the line if you have additional players and give the passer the option of passing to either side. Another variation to this drill is to give the player receiving the pass the option of making a wall pass or faking the wall pass and going past the defender 1v1.

As players get better, or if you have a team with a higher level of skill, you can challenge the players by having all passes be one-touch. This requires much more precision, as the passes must be played at the proper pace, direction, and distance.

Player B passes to player C and plays passive defense before replacing player C. Wall player W runs to be a wall for player C to make a wall pass.

Player C passes to Wall player W and runs around player B to receive a wall pass.

After receiving a wall pass from player W, player C passes to player A, continues running toward him to play passive defense, and then replaces him at the end of the line. Wall player runs to the other end of the line to receive a wall pass from player A.

It's much harder to hit a moving target than a stationary one. It's also considerably harder to hit a moving target with a moving object! Now that your players have been drilled on the fundamental stage of the game, we must move on to the *match-related level*. Match-related means drills that closely approximate the *pressure* of a game.

4. **The King drill.** Start off by dividing the team into pairs, with each pair sharing one ball. Make sure that you block off the goal area with cones and keep it *off limits* for safety. Now, on half of the field have the players with the balls begin to dribble in and around all of the other dribblers and defenders. (The dribblers are all dribbling in and out of one another and their partners.) The players without the balls are also moving all over the field, taking mental pictures of continually changing spaces created by the movement of players. The dribbler will not pass the ball until he is ready, and only then will he pass to *his* partner. This means that he should make eye contact with his partner, indicating "here it comes." If he cannot do that, he shouldn't pass. The ball must be passed on the ground. The partner without the ball must not make a run for the ball into space until eye contact signals that his partner is ready to pass.

This exercise helps alleviate two of the most frustrating problems that are shared by coaches and players alike: (1) when a player is not ready to pass and rushes his pass anyway, it usually is a poor pass—it may be too hard, too soft, or inaccurate; and (2) when a player without the ball makes a run to receive a pass but the player with the ball can't pass it (he isn't looking, he is being pressured by a defender, etc.), the running player simply wastes energy.

Youngsters must be taught that offensively there are only two reasons a player without the ball should be running: (1) to receive a pass and (2) to make space.

Finally, remember that this exercise is an excellent conditioner as well as an exercise to improve skills.

Here are some ways to adapt this exercise:

(1) Have the dribblers pass only with the inside of the foot; then the outside of the foot; then the right foot; then the left foot; then have them alternate feet with each touch.

(2) The passer must pass the ball in less than *four touches.*

(3) The receiver must also receive with different parts of each foot.

(4) Every third or fourth time a player receives the ball it must be played with one touch.

(5) At the blow of the whistle, the player with the ball attacks his partner and tries to dribble by him.

In between these drill changes have your players rest by passing balls back and forth, tossing air balls to one another, or juggling without running.

5. **A variation: The King III.** Divide players into groups of three, providing one ball per group, and have them continue to move as they did with single partners. The dribbler may pass to either of his two partners in the group, who in turn passes to the third partner. Here are a few additional variations:

(1) The first player passes to a partner who must one-touch it to the third partner.

(2) On the whistle, the partners without the ball attack against the third partner.

(3) Have players make their first two passes 5 to 10 yards long and the third pass 20 yards long.

(4) Have the receiver let the ball go by him to the second receiver who is running behind (dummy).

PASSING DRILLS AGAINST PRESSURE

Now that you have done a number of passing/possession drills without defense, the kids are getting confident, passing well, and keeping their heads up. Let's add some defensive pressure (very light—go only about half speed), and try to develop their ability to execute the skills more quickly and when under some pressure. Expect there to be breakdowns on offense. Most kids will get excited as soon as someone challenges them and they have the ball. It's important to stress how crucial it is for them to play with their heads up and know what they are going to do with the ball *before* they get it. If they wait until they receive the ball, they will most likely be under defensive pressure and have difficulty keeping possession.

2v1

This is a very basic drill. Place two players on offense and one player on defense. (like Monkey in the Middle.) The two offensive players move inside a 15-yard by 15-yard grid area. Use cones to make this grid area, and make the area smaller or larger as needed—larger if their skills are weak and they need more room; smaller if their skills are better in order to challenge them. The offensive players pass the ball back and forth and try to make as many passes in a row as they can. The defender should try to steal the ball, then give it back, and the drill starts again.

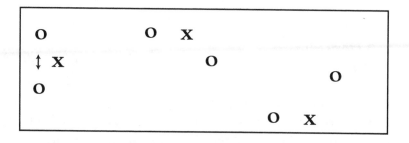

The offensive players should keep the ball moving at all times. When a player receives the ball, he should redirect it away from the defender and create space to give himself time to make a good pass to his teammate. It is also important to remind the player with the ball that good players always play the ball *before* they are in trouble, not after.

The offensive player without the ball is the key. Many young players will just stand in one spot with their hands up and yell, "I'm open!" When this happens, the defender is able to get between the two offensive players and intercept the pass. The receiver must always be moving to a position on either side of the defender so the defender is not in the "passing lane." In this way, the player with the ball has a target and can pass it into space to the receiver.

Some variations for this drill are:

1. The offensive player who loses the ball—by a bad pass or losing possession of the ball—becomes the new defender.

2. If the defender steals the ball, he gets to keep it until the offensive players steal it back.

3. After a defender steals the ball two or three times, change defenders.

3v1

Various soccer studies have shown that during a soccer game, each player has to make up to three hundred independent decisions. These decisions range from who they should pass the ball to along with when and how, the person they should defend and how, when they should attack. . . . The decisions are endless, as you can see. In this drill, players must make some of the decisions that are required in each game.

Use the same size grid as the 2v1 exercise. If your team is not large, you can also use the center circle and rotate groups into the circle. This drill will help to reinforce in players the need to keep their heads up and make good decisions.

One player should start with the ball. The other two offensive players move to the sides of this player and into good positions to receive the ball. As with the 2v1 drill, the defender tries to steal the ball, and you may use the same variations for rotating defenders into this drill as well.

To start out, pretend that the players are playing in a square. The person with the ball is in one corner, and the other offensive players are in the corners to either side of this player. As the offensive player with the ball is challenged by the defender he keeps his head up and can easily see which player and side the defender is favoring. He then simply passes the ball to the other offensive player (Diagram A).

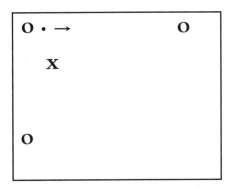

A

Once the second offensive player receives the ball, the other offensive players must immediately move to get on either side of that person for "support." They re-create the "square" with a person on either side of the ball, and the drill continues (Diagram B).

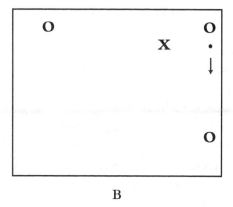

B

Once again, the players without the ball are the key. They have to make certain that the defender is not in the passing lane between them and the player with the ball. The receivers may have to move toward the player with the ball and slightly right or left to receive the ball.

FULL TEAM DRILLS

1. **King four ball.** Bring the entire group together. Inform the players that now they don't have any partners and can pass and receive with anyone. Provide only four balls. As the players pass and move, remind them that they can't yell or say anything. *If they want to receive a pass, they must ask for it by sprinting into a space.*

2. **Keepaway.** Divide players into two separate teams. Use one half of the field and one ball. *The object of keepaway is for one team to make ten passes in a row before the other team steals the ball away and makes ten passes in a row.* The passes must be at least 5 yards, and two players cannot make more than three passes between themselves. If one team makes three passes in a row and loses the ball to the other team, they give immediate chase (first rule of defense) to steal the ball back. If

they can steal the ball back before the other team completes a pass, they continue counting from three. If one pass has been completed, however, they must go back to zero.

There are a few variations that can be used for this game, too:

(1) Allow each player only two touches, then three touches, then many touches with the ball.

(2) Allow players to use only their right foot or left foot, or the inside or outside of their kicking foot.

(3) *"Many touches one-touch"*: Teams play keepaway by alternating one-touch and then many touches between players of the same team. This challenges both the passer and the receiver. The player touching the ball many times knows that the teammate he passes to must one-touch the ball, so the ball must be passed with the proper pace. The receiver who is going to receive the pass to be one-touched must know what he is going to do with the ball before he touches. The receiver, therefore, must take "pictures" of the spaces around him, and be aware of defenders and teammates, in order to know where the ball should be passed with one touch.

(4) In the *"short/short/long game,"* players make two consecutive short passes between 5 and 10 yards and a third pass of at least 20 yards to the other side of the field. One point is given each time the task is completed. Youth soccer players are inclined to bunch up! We call this *Beehive Soccer*. This drill teaches your players to move the ball from one side of the field to the other and to keep space between them and their teammates. (See diagram on next page.)

One way to teach this is the first time two players bunch up, stop play. Then ask them if they realize the defender can mark both of them because they are so close!

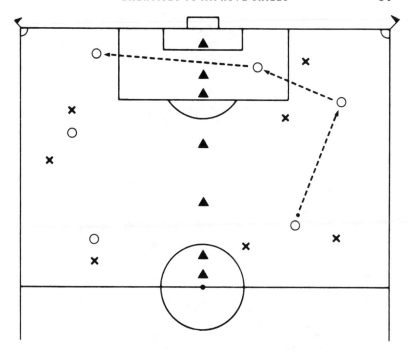

In each of these exercises, variations or gimmicks can be added to focus on any specific problems your team may have. Don't be afraid to experiment with the drill changes. It will help to improve play and should prove to be fun.

You'll find your kids will love *"Go for goal."* Most of the exercises in this chapter can be modified to allow the players to "go for goal." For example, if your team is playing keepaway, yell, "Go for goal!" every few minutes. The team in possession of the ball has ten seconds in which to score a goal. Use only one goal. The defending team must quickly *"mark up"* (guard) a man and try to stop the offensive team from scoring.

Finally, try this for real fun: *"Close your eyes."* Using the drills mentioned above—keepaway, for example—yell for the player to close his eyes when he receives a ball. Now ask him to tell you where two of his teammates (possible receivers) are located. If he can't tell you where they are, it means that he didn't take mental pictures of their locations before he received the ball. Remind him that the

passer must know what he is going to do with the ball before he receives it. Some players will be able to tell you not only where players
are but also who they are.

At this point in practice talk to your players again and reinforce
the importance of not kicking the ball far downfield in a soccer
game. That's not soccer—that's kickball.

Let's look at why kickball is popular. Coaches will sometimes
play their fastest, most skilled players as forwards. By the time they
finish selecting their midfielders and eventually select their backs, the
only players left are the smallest, slowest, or least skilled. The players

designated as backs, as well as their coach, are petrified that a mistake will occur and the opposing forwards will race in and score a goal. So the coach instructs them to "kick it out," and the backs become good kickers but very poor soccer players. As a result, the game evolves into one large kickball game played between backs and forwards as the midfielders watch the ball being kicked back and forth over their heads.

What can be done about kickball? First, teach your backs to never kick the ball "out" unless it is in a dangerous position in front of their goal. When this occurs and the backs try to "clear it," the rules are: get height (even if it goes straight up, the goalie can out-jump anyone by using his hands); clear the ball to the side; and, finally, get distance. Remind them that if they have time to do all three, they probably had time to settle the ball and pass it out to a teammate and begin to attack. Every time a player kicks the ball "out," the defending team has the chance to regain possession and attack again. So, remember the cardinal rule and teach it to your backs: *Maintain possession of the ball.* Don't give it up. Don't be in a rush to go straight downfield to score a goal. The other team may well have more players back on defense than you do on offense in a certain part of the field. As a result, it may be necessary to attack by passing (not kicking) to another part of the field where your team has numerical superiority.

A final comment to make to your team regarding passing is to reassert the importance of maintaining possession of the ball. Point to the soccer goal on your field and say to your players, "That is the goal we are going for. We don't care how long it takes, but we want to arrive there and with the ball." The team holding the ball the longest usually is the winner. Your team's attitude should be, "Once we get it, we want to keep it."

RECEIVING

Many coaches give little thought to the skill of *getting* the ball as opposed to passing it. We believe you must not only teach the art of receiving but practice it constantly.

REMEMBER THE RULE: RECEIVING THE BALL IN SOCCER ALWAYS LEADS TO SOMETHING ELSE: MOVING AWAY WITH IT, SHIELDING IT, PASSING IT, OR SHOOTING IT.

The exercises that follow are designed to provide a progression for your players to learn receiving.

1. **Stationary reception.** In the first exercise, toss balls to each player, who will practice receiving them with the *sole of the foot, instep, inside and outside of the foot, thigh, chest, and head.* After your players are handling most of the tosses comfortably, add pressure to make it more game-related.

Remember, game-related means adding pressure that more closely simulates what your young people will actually experience in a game.

2. **Toss and attack.** Have the players pair up. One partner tosses the ball. When the receiver touches the ball, the tosser immediately attacks to steal the ball. He has five seconds to pull off the steal. Then the players switch roles. The partners should practice receiving the ball with all parts of the body.

3. **Toss and move to space.** Next, have the server toss a ball and run into a different space. The receiver must control the ball, then find his partner and pass it to him; or, as a variation, have the receivers one-touch the ball back to the server.

4. **Bull in ring.** Group your players into fours, combining the sets of pairs already set up. Three of the players each have a ball and form a 15-yard triangle around the fourth player, who is the receiver. The receiver handles a pass from one server, controls it, and returns it with two touches to the same server. Then the receiver takes a pass from the next player, returns it, and finally repeats this drill with the third player. The drill is repeated five times. In the first four rounds the players toss the balls, in turn, to the foot, thigh, chest, and head. In

the fifth round the ball is directed anywhere! The players rotate after each completed round.

5. **Defender at the D.** Group your players in threes around a goal. One player tosses high balls to a receiver who is standing at the penalty arc (D). A defender stands behind the receiver playing low pressure. (Low pressure means staying with the player but not trying to take the ball away.) The receiver controls the ball and turns for a shot. As the receiver becomes more proficient, the defender increases pressure, eventually giving the maximum challenge. When the receiver can't make the turn to shoot, he may pass it back to the server.

DRIBBLING, DRIVING, SHIELDING

REMEMBER THE RULES:
1. CHANGE SPEED
2. CHANGE DIRECTION
3. KEEP THE HEAD UP

THE ONLY TIME A PLAYER HAS HIS HEAD DOWN IS WHEN HE FIRST TOUCHES THE BALL AND WHEN HE LAST TOUCHES THE BALL.

1. **Creative dribbling.** You need to set up a grid for the first dribbling exercise.

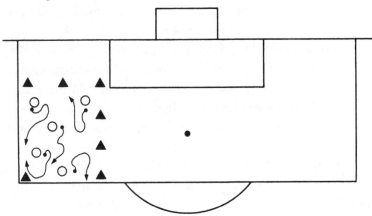

The size of your grid depends on the number of players you want in the drill and their level of skill. Every player starts with a ball. (If you don't have enough balls to go around, pair up the players, each member of each pair taking turns with a ball.) Direct your players to begin dribbling, also telling them you will raise your fist when you want them to stop. This will force your dribblers to keep their heads up. The players stop the ball by lightly stepping on the ball with their feet.

First, have everyone dribble only with the right foot. Then the left. Then the inside of both feet. Then the outside of both feet. These changes ensure that each player learns to use all parts of the foot. Continually remind everyone to change direction and speed, as well as to dribble with the head up.

2. **Whistle drill.** Using the same rules, have your players dribble wherever they wish. When you blow the whistle, each player must pick up his ball with his hands before you blow the whistle again. Vary the time between the first and second whistle. Then you're controlling the ball. Remember, head up!

Use the same grid for Exercises 3 and 4.

3. **King of the hill.** In this exercise, players must dribble their balls nonstop. Instruct them that the drill requires each player to knock the other players' balls out of the grid with their feet, like a big game of marbles. Any balls knocked out of the grid may fly no higher than cone height. This ensures that the players use controlled, directed taps to knock out other balls. Whoever remains in the grid with their ball at the end is the winner.

4. **Shadow dribbling.** Pair up your players for this exercise. One partner takes the ball and dribbles all over the field, executing one-on-one (1v1) moves. The other partner follows behind and imitates his moves. This is a good way for players to learn moves from one another. After a minute or so of the activity, have the partners switch responsibilities.

5. **Eight Mini-Goals 1v1.** In a 30-yard by 30-yard grid area, set up between eight to ten sets of cones, with each set approximately 3 yards apart. The number of cones you use will depend upon the

number of players on the team and the size of the area available. Adjust the number of cones you use if you have too many or too few players or if the size of the area is not appropriate for the team.

Try to pair off partners according to how fast they are (don't mention this to your players to avoid hurting feelings). Everyone on the team goes at once. Remind them that they must keep their heads up when dribbling as they would in a game to avoid collisions and to see which goal is not blocked by other players or by their defensive partner.

One partner starts with the ball and attempts to score a goal. A goal is scored when a player dribbles through any of the pairs of cones and maintains possession of the ball. If he loses control of the ball or pass or shoots it through the goal, it is not a goal. The player with the ball keeps it for 30 seconds and tries to score as many goals as possible during that time period. If she loses it, the defending partner gives it back immediately.

After 30 seconds ask the players how many goals they scored. Then have the first defensive player start with the ball and count the number of goals she scores for 30 seconds. Repeat this drill with both players one more time. After that, give the ball to the partner who scored the fewest goals. Now, however, if the player loses the ball, the defending player gets to keep the ball until it is stolen back. Continue for about thirty seconds and start another round after giving the ball to the person who scored the fewest goals.

O— OFFENDER
X— DEFENDER

6. 1v1/Two goal. The next exercise is one-on-one (1v1) through either of two goals. Set up two one-yard-wide goals with cones 10 yards apart. Ten yards away, in front of the goals, is an attacker with the ball. The attacker tries to dribble through either of the two goals before the defender steals the ball. The players switch after the attempt.

7. 1v1/Two goal counter. The only difference here is that we now have another set of one-yard-wide goals on either side of the attacker. The attacker starts and if the defender steals the ball, he immediately counterattacks and the attacker must play defense.

8. 2v2/Two goal. Using the same goal setup, have players pair up as two attackers and two defenders. Increase the grid area from 10 yards by 10 yards to 15 yards wide by 20 yards long. Now a 2v2 situation is presented with the same attack and counterattack rules.

9. Dribbling over the line game. Playing across half of the field, one team tries to score a goal by dribbling over the sideline. The ball cannot be passed but must be dribbled over the line to score a goal.

10. Steal the Bacon. Set up a grid 20 yards by 20 yards (adjust the size for the age and skill level of the players—larger for less skilled, smaller for more skilled). Split the players into two teams with an equal number on each side. Have the players stand facing one another behind the line on opposite sides of the grid. Now pair up each player on one team with a player on the other team and give them the same number. If possible, try to match them up by ability. If you have one team with one less player, assign one player on that team to be two numbers.

The game begins with the coach calling out one number and can start in any number order. The player on each side with that number runs out and tries to gain possession of the ball. Once he gains possession, he tries to dribble the ball back to his sideline. The player scores a goal by stopping the ball within 6 inches of his line with the top of his foot for one second. The player without the ball tries to steal the ball away from this player. If he does, he dribbles it back to his side and tries to stop it on his line.

Once a goal is scored, the players return to their sides and the coach calls out a different number to come out. Sometimes players may find it difficult to score. In that case, give the players no more than thirty seconds to score, stop play, and call another number. Don't forget to make sure that you call every number one time before calling out a number a second time.

Some strategy can be used in this exercise. The player with the ball may decide not to try to dribble past the defender but, instead, pass the ball to someone on his line. If he tries to score using this tactic, the passer must continue moving toward the ball as his teammate on the line can only *one-touch* the ball back to him.

A variation of this exercise is for the coach to call out a player's number, and that player must then call out a second number to help him create a 2v2 situation. When this happens, the goal cannot be scored until both players have touched the ball.

Another variation of this exercise is for the coach to call out two or even three numbers and create the 2v2 or 3v3 situations.

SHIELDING EXERCISES

Shielding. A technique to help players keep possession of the ball is shielding. When a player has control of the ball and stands sideways between the ball and the defender, he is shielding the ball. If he turns his back to the defender and cannot see him, he loses the opportunity to use any of those tactics. When he stands sideways, he is wider and can keep the defender a greater distance away from the ball. He can also see the defender, his teammates, and the goal. This will allow him to make a decision as to whether he should attack the defender, pass the ball to a teammate, or shoot at the goal.

1. **Five-second shield.** In the first exercise, one player stands sideways between the ball and his partner. No one touches the ball. The player closest to the ball tries to shield his partner from the ball for five seconds as the defender tries to step on top of the ball. Encourage the shielding player to stay low and lean into his partner with his shoulder. After three tries, switch places.

2. **1v1 Keepaway.** Set up a 25-yard by 25-yard grid for the next exercise. Have everyone pair up and stand in the grid. One player is on offense and the other on defense. The exercise begins with the defender trying to steal the ball from the shielding offensive player. If the defender steals the ball from his partner, he gives it back and immediately tries for another steal. After a minute of this, stop and ask for the players who made it through the exercise without having their ball stolen to raise their hands. A variation of this exercise allows the defender to keep the ball if he steals it. Then the offensive player must try to steal it back.

3. **Team shielding.** In the next exercise, the grid remains the same but the players dribbling the ball must try to shield from everyone. Anyone without a ball can steal from any other player with a ball. In this exercise it's wise to take away a few balls to increase the number of defenders.

4. **How many?** This last shielding exercise forces the players dribbling the ball to keep their heads up and, at the same time, protect the ball from a defender. Players are paired up again with one ball. The players shield from one another inside the grid. When a

player steals the ball, he keeps it. After a while yell, "How many?" At that moment, the players shielding the ball must look up and shout out the number of fingers being held up. When the shielder is occupied with calling out the number, the defender can attempt a steal.

9

GOALKEEPING

Goalkeepers are very special people, and as a result they need special training to develop.

Unfortunately, many coaches consider their goalkeepers to be defenders only. This just isn't true. Goalkeepers not only *defend* the goal but must *support* all of their teammates and actually start the *attack*. Goalkeepers are *offensive* players, too! It is important to get this across to your goalkeepers and field players.

Goalkeeping is physically and emotionally demanding. It's a good idea, therefore, for all of your team to experience the unique feeling of working in front of the net. Give each player a chance in goal, and attitudes and perspectives will change.

Some field players might be upset with the goalkeeper because he gave up the goal. Place the complainer in the goal so he can see how difficult it can be. Remember what was said earlier: no one is allowed to say anything negative to a goalkeeper after a score has occurred. Explain that before the ball got by the goalkeeper, it got by ten other players! The right wing may have lost the ball to a defender and not given immediate chase. The midfielder may not have marked the most dangerous man and enabled a more dangerous player to get free. A back may have run out of control and been beaten by the player with the ball. Finally, the ball has reached the goal and the shooter made a great shot. Can the goalkeeper really be blamed for this goal?

A goalkeeper should keep track of all the goals scored against him. Keeping a log of how the goal was scored, what he did, what the shooter did, and what he should do differently next time (if anything) will help the goalkeeper understand his strengths and weaknesses. Then, in practice, work with him and watch for a pattern to the goals scored against him. Perhaps he needs help with high balls, balls to his left or right, or his agility. Writing down this information *now* will lead to less writing in the *future*.

Communication. It is very important to have communication between all players, especially with the goalkeeper. When a ball is passed toward the goal, the goalkeeper must communicate to his teammates what he is doing or what they should do. Two basic calls that he must make are "Keeper!" and "Away!" Quite often the goalkeeper will need to make his call more than once to make certain that his teammates have heard him. If the goalkeeper yells "Keeper!" this means he is going to get the ball, and field players should give him room. (However, the defenders must still stay with their man in the event the goalkeeper mishandles the ball.) If the goalkeeper yells "Away!" this means that the goalkeeper is not going to play the ball and the field players must clear the ball away from the goal. If nothing is said, the field player must play the ball and assume that the goalkeeper cannot get to the ball.

The Goalkeeper: How and Where to Stand. The goalkeeper must be ready to defend an attack at a moment's notice. Sometimes young goalkeepers may be seen picking flowers in front of the goal or doing cartwheels and caught by surprise! There are a few ways to keep goalkeepers awake in the goal, and we will go over those later in this chapter.

First, let's talk about how the goalkeeper should be standing. As with most sports, the goalkeeper should be in an athletic position when he sees an opponent preparing to attack. This means feet shoulder-width apart, knees flexed, and weight on the balls of the feet. It is very important for the goalkeeper to always stay balanced. As the ball moves from side to side on the field, the goalkeeper must keep turning his body back and forth while moving his feet to keep facing the ball. He cannot just turn his head from side to side.

Once the goalkeeper is in a balanced position, he should have his hands facing forward toward the ball with his palms down approximately waist height in a relaxed manner. In this position, the hands will have to travel only half the distance to save a high ball or low ball. Some goalkeepers may prefer to stand in a slightly different position. They may crouch lower to the ground, similar to a basketball player playing defense with his hands down at his sides and his palms facing the ball. The downside to this position, however, is that you have farther to move your hands to save a high ball.

Once he is in the ready position and a shot is taken, the goalkeeper should move his body so that he is directly behind the ball. This creates a second barrier to help prevent the ball from going into the goal. If he misses the save with his hands, his body will be in a position to block the ball. If the ball is mishandled and not caught, he still has a chance to make the save.

So, now that you know how to stand, you need to know where to stand.

One of the worst things a goalkeeper can do is just stand in front of the goal for the entire game. The goalkeeper needs to move forward and backward and side to side in front of the goal, just like the field players do when running up and down the field. Moving in such a manner gives the goalkeeper an opportunity to communicate with his teammates throughout the game as well as keep himself and his teammates alert. The goalkeeper must focus on all of the players and know where the ball is at all times.

To determine how far the goalkeeper should come away from the goal, he should break the soccer field into thirds—offensive third, middle third, and defensive third. In the same way, he should divide the area from the goal line to the top of the penalty area into thirds.

When the ball is in the offensive third of the field, the goalkeeper should be at the top of the penalty area (18-yard line). In this position, he will be able to intercept any long passes that come into the penalty area before a shot can be taken. If the goalkeeper has to come outside of the penalty area to beat an attacking player to the ball, he must be certain not to use his hands and just kick or head the ball away like a field player.

When the ball is in the middle third of the field, the goalkeeper should retreat and stand between the penalty spot (12-yard spot) and the top of the 6-yard goal area.

Finally, when the ball is in the defensive third of the field, the goal-keeper should back up inside the 6-yard goal area. A taller goalkeeper can stand approximately 2 to 3 yards off the goal line. A shorter goal-keeper should stand approximately 1 yard off the goal line to have a better chance to stop high balls that drop just under the crossbar.

Some goalkeepers seem to make one incredible save after another in a game. Her play looks spectacular. Fans are cheering her acrobat-ics. While it is possible that she has the ability to become an incredi-ble goalkeeper, it is also possible that at the moment she is a very poor one. Those incredible saves may just be a result of not playing the angles and being out of position. Good goalkeepers are excellent at *angle* play, which means narrowing the gap at which the ball can enter the goal.

Playing the angle correctly allows the goalie to place himself di-rectly in front of the player taking a shot.

One way to cut off the shooting angles toward goal is for the goalie to pretend the ball is a flashlight pointed at the goal. The goalie walks out to the flashlight until his shadow covers the goal. He has cut off angles to the left and right.

When the ball is being shot from the side of the goal, the goalie should position himself in front of the goal and between the two posts.

A good way to check if the goalie is centered properly is to have a few balls placed in an arc about 18 yards away from the goal.

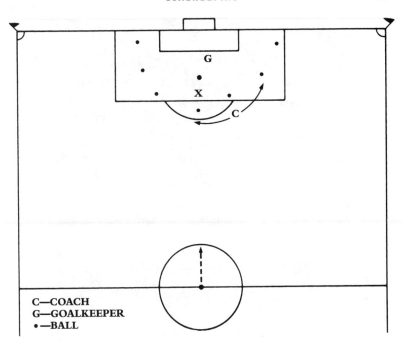

C—COACH
G—GOALKEEPER
•—BALL

The coach should stand behind a ball and have the goalkeeper position himself where he thinks he should be in relation to that ball. Then the goalie can place a towel or his gloves where he was standing and come out to the coach. You can also have a second player stand where the goalkeeper was standing and then have the goalkeeper come out. Both coach and player can now check together to see if the angle was covered, and your keeper will know right away how he did. Take a look at the following photos. See how our goalie has cut off the angle in each photo? You may want to show this page to all your goalkeepers.

To cut off the angle on the high ball, the goalkeeper should play as far in front of the goal as he likes as long as shots on goal can't go over his head and into the goal. How far out each keeper plays will depend on individual speed, quickness, reaction, and judgment. You and the goalies can find this out only in practice. So, shoot balls at them from various distances as they find out just how far out they can come and not get beaten.

As soon as the goalkeeper has the ball in his hands, he must start the *attack*. Teach your goalkeeper to look to the opposite side of the field from where the ball was shot. Whenever possible, he should throw or roll the ball out to a field player, which will assure your team a better chance to maintain possession of the ball. When the ball is punted out, the other team will wind up with the ball half the time. There are times, however, when you would want your goalkeeper to punt: if a strong wind or the sun is at his back; if your opponents have very weak backs and you have quicker forwards; if you're losing late in the game; if your opponents are caught up on attack and your deepest man has a 1v1 with a back; or if your backs are weak and having trouble passing the ball and building the attack.

Catch It. Okay, so now we know how to stand, where to stand, and what to say. But what do we do when a shot or pass is made toward the goal? The safest place for a soccer ball is in the goalkeeper's hands. The goalkeeper should try to *catch* every ball he can. Only if he cannot catch it should he try to deflect it or punch it away. Emphasize to your goalkeepers that they haven't made a save until the ball is in their hands and then passed or kicked to a teammate to start the attack. Knocking the ball down or blocking the shot only constitutes the first part of the save. The good goalkeeper quickly gets back off the ground, finds the ball again, and controls it. (The poor ones will usually have to turn around and get the ball out of the back of the net.)

Saving shots below the waist. Many of the saves that the goal-keeper will have to make will be below the waist. On this type of shot, the goalkeeper should stand with her feet close enough together that the ball can't slip through her legs and go into the goal.

She should hold her palms open with her fingers pointing toward the ball. As the save is made, the ball rolls onto the hands and up the forearms, and then is brought up to the chest as the goalkeeper stands up.

Another way to make this type of save is for the goalkeeper to slightly bend one of her knees behind her body and then bend forward at the waist, making the save the same way as the straight-leg save.

Saving shots at waist height. Saving a shot at waist height is similar to making a save below the waist. The goalkeeper should move directly behind the shot, making sure that her knees are flexed and she is balanced. She begins the save by bending at the waist with her forearms facing the ball and elbows even with the hips, catching the ball between the heel of the palm and the wrists. She should give slightly at the waist as contact is made, roll the ball up to the chest, and hold it against the chest with the forearms and hands.

Saving high balls—Shots and Passes. Saving high balls requires the save be made with the hands. As with other saves, the goalkeeper must center his body behind the ball. The hands must be in front of the goalkeeper's head in a "W" formation. (This means that the goalkeeper spreads his fingers with his thumbs behind the ball and his other fingers to the sides of the ball.) The first contact with the ball is made with the fingertips. The goalkeeper should cushion the ball by giving when contact is made (slightly bending the wrists and hands back). By giving and cushioning the ball, the goalkeeper helps to prevent the ball from hitting the hands too hard and bouncing away.

When a shot or pass toward the goal is well above the goalkeeper's head, she may have to jump into the air to catch it. This will require some judgment on her part. The goalkeeper should take small steps toward the ball before taking one big step to jump up for the ball. She wants to catch the ball at the peak of her jump while directly facing the ball. The jump should be made off of one foot while bringing up one knee and both arms to get as much lift as possible. Lifting up one knee (the one farthest from the ball) will also protect the goalkeeper's ribs from a charging attacker. The jumping motion should be similar to a basketball ball player jumping off one foot to dunk a basketball with two hands.

Shuffle Drill. Goalkeepers must be able to move forward, backward, up, down, and especially sideways. If a goalkeeper can't move sideways, he will have difficulty getting his body behind the ball to make a save when a shot is taken. He will move backward to turn around and get the opponent's shot out of the goal! In order to move sideways, the goalkeeper should start in a balanced position and learn to take short, lateral shuffle steps without crossing his legs.

At the same time, goalkeepers must also learn the size of the goal and how quickly and how far they have to move in order to stop any ball from getting past them. The shuffle drill is a great drill to help them learn that.

First, have the goalkeeper stand on the 6-yard line in front of the center of the goal with her eyes closed. Then, have a coach stand in front of each goalpost. You'll see why in a moment. Have your goalkeeper try to take shuffle steps in an arc pattern. Once the goalkeeper thinks she is at the post, have her open up her eyes to see how close she is. In most cases, the goalkeeper will be well short of the post and realize just how large the goal is—24 feet! Have her try it again and then try going to the left side. Eventually, have her try to go to the right and then immediately back to the left.

Delivering the ball—starting the attack. All goalkeepers must learn to throw and punt. As previously mentioned, there are times when the goalkeeper should punt the ball. Whenever a punt is taken, however, the other team will often gain possession. Whenever possible, the goalie should throw the ball to a teammate because it is easier to control and will help your team maintain possession. Your goalie may need both hands to bring the soccer ball back to the throwing position.

As he brings the ball over the throwing shoulder, he should spread his fingers, step forward, and throw. Teach him to snap his hand straight down on the follow-through as if he were throwing a baseball.

When your goalie practices punting, have him concentrate first of all on striking the center of the ball on the laces. Then these are the steps: (1) point the toe and lock the ankle; and (2) drop the ball on the foot—don't throw it in the air and hope to kick it.

Have your goalies practice this technique by standing 10 yards apart and punting back and forth. Gradually move them apart until they are punting for distance. This is also good practice for catching high balls.

You can devise any number of exercises for the goalkeeper. He can throw balls up in the air to himself, then sit down, or kneel, roll, or do a push-up, quickly get up, and catch the ball. Anything that forces him to move and catch balls from different positions and an-

gles is great. It will help his agility and quickness and make him a better goalkeeper.

Two important rules regarding goalkeeping were amended by FIFA in 1997. These are important for your goalkeepers and field players to know. In the first situation, if a field player deliberately kicks the ball back to his own goalkeeper, the goalkeeper is not permitted to touch the ball with his hands but may control it with his feet and pass it or kick it away. If, however, the goalkeeper does touch the ball with his hands, he is penalized with an indirect free kick being taken by the opposing team from wherever on the field he touched the ball with his hands. A field player may pass the ball back to the goalkeeper with his head, chest, or knee. In these situations, the goalkeeper may catch the ball with his hands.

The second change involves the goalkeeper holding on to the ball too long. If the referee believes that the goalkeeper is wasting time and holding on to the ball for longer than six seconds before releasing it, he can call a penalty. This sometimes occurs late in the game when the goalkeeper's team has a lead and he may well be trying to waste time. An indirect free kick is awarded to the opposing team if the referee makes this call.

As stated, the goalkeeper is a special player. He is also an equal member of your team and should be treated as such. The coach must find ways each practice to incorporate him into the training session. The goalie must learn his teammates' strengths and weaknesses, and they, his. It is important to incorporate him into the various shooting exercises and offensive and defensive tactical exercises that have been discussed.

10
OFFENSIVE TACTICS

Soccer is a game of opposites. The offensive team stretches itself across the field to gain width and depth as a team. The defensive team tries to condense itself. At the same time the attackers are trying to outnumber and penetrate the defense, their opponents are trying to get more players back to defend their goal. A creative offense can overrun and penetrate the defense as players improvise to find a way to get the ball into the net.

A soccer game really isn't made up of two teams playing 11v11. It really is made up of opportunities to create 1v1 and 2v1 attacks all over the field with a third player as a receiver, an overlapping player, or a player in some type of supporting role.

Attacking. When attacking, the player with the ball should face his offensive goal and look for the *deepest* teammate. If he can play a ball to that player, he should. This *penetration pass* cuts through the defense and immediately leaves a pack of defenders behind the ball. If it is too risky to play a ball directly forward, the player should look to play a ball *diagonally*. If this is also too risky, your player must look to pass a square ball out to the side or behind him to a supporting player. Any pass played square or backward is considered a *possession pass*. Since penetration passes are risky, always have your offense possess the ball until it can find a weaker area to attack. Your most important concern as a coach is for your players to maintain possession of the ball. Remember: in a soccer game, one team plays soccer and the other team chases. If you give up the ball, you have to chase.

When a player has an opportunity to attack, he needs be able to beat the defender and create an opportunity for himself or a teammate to shoot. Every attacking player needs to be able to dribble past a defender going to the right or going to the left. It can be the same move to each side. It can also be a double move that starts out like the first move so that the defender thinks the same move is being made. However, after showing the first move, the player takes the ball in the opposite direction.

A player must also have a change-of-direction move. This is a move where the player starts in one direction down the field and tries to beat a defender. Once he realizes that he can't beat the defender going in one direction, he makes a quick move to turn back toward the original direction.

The exercises listed below will greatly improve the touch and balance of your players and are great homework assignments. As your players are doing these exercises in practice, pick out a few players who excel and have them demonstrate to the team. Kids like to be in the spotlight, and this is great incentive for them to practice at home—to give themselves a chance to demonstrate at the next practice.

BEING ONE WITH THE BALL

Players must acquire a feel for the soccer ball before they can develop the ability to attack a defender. This is similar to a basketball player learning how to dribble a ball with his head up or eyes closed and trying to feel the ball with his fingertips. Once the player feels like the ball is attached to his foot, he can confidently move with it and attack players when necessary.

The more times a player has contact with the ball, the better her touch will become. That's why we recommend that every player have a ball at practice.

Here are a series of exercises designed to develop feel with the ball combined with exercises of *active rest*. After doing a strenuous drill, many coaches have their players take a break, relax, sit around, and talk. *Active rest* exercises are opportunities to develop greater touch with the ball while at the same time challenging the players while they are a little fatigued. This challenge is similar to players having to execute skills late in a game when they are tired.

1. **Fast Footwork.** Each player stands with the ball between his feet. As he jogs in place, he gently taps the ball back and forth with the inside of his foot. Watch carefully, and you will find that the majority of your players will try to tap the ball back and forth with straight, stiff legs. Do not allow them to do that. Have them pretend that they are just jogging with bent knees, then with each step they tap the ball to the other foot. Do this for about 30 seconds and stop. Repeat.

2. Active Rest—Circles. Have the players stand on one foot while placing the bottom of the other foot on top of the ball. The players then make circles clockwise and counterclockwise on top of the ball with the ball of their foot. This exercise also helps to develop balance on one foot. They can alternate feet and make large and small circles to mix things up.

3. Fast Footwork Forward. Each player starts with fast footwork again and moves a short distance forward after each tap for about 5 yards, turns, and comes back the same way to the starting point. Every tap is a step forward.

4. Active Rest—Roll Downs. Facing the ball, players put their right foot on top of the ball and roll the inside of their right foot down the outside of the ball. Then, with their right foot on the ground put their left foot on top of the ball and roll the inside of their left foot down the outside of the ball. The foot must remain in contact with the ball the entire time and will move only a few inches. Repeat rotating about five times to each side.

5. Fast Footwork—Roll Downs. The player starts with fast footwork while jogging in place. After three or four taps, he puts his right foot on top of the ball and rolls his right foot down the outside of the ball until his foot hits the ground. The player does fast footwork again and after three or four taps, rolls his left foot down the outside of the ball until his foot touches the ground. Continue alternating for 30 seconds.

6. Active Rest—Slide the foot. The player stands at a 45-degree angle to the ball with the bottom of his foot on top of the ball. He slides his foot forward and backward over the ball from his toe to his heel. The foot must remain in contact with the ball at all times and will move only a few inches. Repeat and use both feet.

7. **Fast Footwork—Clockwork Turns.** Players pretend they are standing on top of the center of a clock facing straight ahead at what would be twelve o'clock. Each player starts with fast footwork. After three or four taps, the player puts his right foot on top of the ball and pulls it back a quarter turn to the right so she is facing what would be three o'clock. The ball moves only a few inches. After three or four fast footwork taps, the player puts his right foot on top of the ball and pulls the ball back a quarter turn facing what would now be six o'clock. Continue to nine o'clock and then back to twelve o'clock. Repeat and try it with the other foot if players have success.

8. **Active Rest—Rollovers.** Each player faces the ball with the inside of his right foot touching the outside of the ball and his left foot slightly behind the ball. *The player must keep his foot in contact with the ball the entire time he does this exercise.* With his toes always facing forward, the player rolls his foot over the ball from the inside of his foot, to the bottom of his foot and, finally, to the outside of his foot. His foot actually passes in front of the left leg before touching the ground. Then he reverses the direction, again with his foot always in contact with the ball from the outside of his foot, to the bottom of his foot, to the inside of his foot. Repeat five times and try this with both feet.

9. **Figure 8's.** Each player begins by standing 2 to 3 inches behind the ball. The player never touches the ball in this exercise. He starts by stepping forward, bringing his right foot toward his left foot as he makes a circle around the ball. He finishes by placing his right foot in front of the left foot. The player returns to the starting position and then takes a few steps in place. He then continues doing the same movement in the other direction, with his left foot going toward his right foot. As the player alternates circling with the right foot and then the left foot, he tries to scrape the ground in front of the ball. Do this five times with each foot and then repeat.

10. **Active Rest—Toe to Knee.** The player faces the ball and stands on his left foot. The toes of the right foot touch the ground, and the laces are touching the back of the ball. *The player must keep his foot in contact with the ball the entire time he does this exercise.* The player raises his right knee and rolls the ball forward as it stays in contact with the foot from laces to toes to bottom of the foot. Return in reverse to the starting point with the toes of the right foot on the ground and the laces touching the ball.

1 V 1 OFFENSIVE EXERCISES

As we mentioned before, attackers must be able to beat defenders to the right and to the left. They can attack much more quickly by **using one foot.** While utilizing the inside and outside of the same foot, a player can make many different feints to throw the defender off balance. The simplest way to attack is by pushing the ball forward and then using a head, shoulder, hip, or leg fake as you are watching the defender. The ball does all the work, and you do not even have to look at it. All you have to do is watch the defender to see which way he is leaning and then go the opposite way with one dribble.

A good way to practice this is with our **Cone-tag** drill.

Line up your players and place one defender 10 yards away in front of two cones that are 5 yards apart. The defender's job is to tag the attacker with two hands. The attacker has five seconds to try to run through the cones without being tagged. No balls are used. After each player attacks, he becomes the defender. By playing without a ball, your players will learn all sorts of fakes with the head, shoulders, hips, and legs. When a player beats the defender by running to one side, ask him why he ran to that side. He will say that he saw the defender lean the opposite way. And how did he know? He had his head up! Now try to do the same drill with the ball. Instruct your players to let the ball do the work, letting it roll as they feint, keeping their heads up and using one foot.

Here are a few simple 1v1 moves that you will see used by the best players in the world, and your players can learn them, too.

1. **The Step-over.** There are two ways to feint and step over a ball: (1) The player's foot may pass over the ball from the outside in; or (2) the player's foot may pass over the ball from the inside out.

   Outside In: If the player steps over the ball with his right foot by stepping toward the left foot, he has stepped from the outside in.

Inside Out: If the player steps over the ball with his right foot going away from his left foot, he is stepping from the inside out.

In both of these movements the ball is moving forward. The player may step behind the ball, over the ball, or around the ball to do the move when she is attacking a defender.

2. **Scissors.** If your players are able to do the step-over, they can have some fun learning the next move, the scissors. Very simply, this is the step-over move done two times in a row, once in each direction. The simplest way to learn this move is to have the attacking player step toward the left side of the ball with his left foot as he fakes going to the left, then step toward the right side of the ball with his right foot as he fakes going to the right, and then fake going to the left again before tapping the ball with the outside of the right foot and moving past the defender to the right. Confusing? Well, here is what we mean. As the player attacks the defender, he should fake tapping the ball with the outside of his left foot as if he were going to dribble the ball to the left. With his next step, the attacker pretends to tap the ball with the outside of his right foot as if he were going to dribble the ball to the right. The final movement is to have the player once again fake a dribble to the left with the outside of his left foot and then, using the outside of the right foot, dribble the ball to the right. You will find that it isn't as hard as it sounds once you know how to do the step-over move first. Be aware that with the scissor move, greater distance is necessary between the attacker and the defender, as the move takes longer to do. As long as the player keeps his head up, he will see the defender, start the move with plenty of time, and not fall over in a tangle of feet and legs!

3. **Fake sole back.** Another effective move for players is the fake

sole back move. Try to visualize a wing dribbling down the sideline in order to cross the ball to a teammate in front of the goal. The defender is with him step for step, and the wing can't seem to get far enough ahead to cross the ball. Try this. Once you get the defender running hard with you, briefly slow down and fake pulling the ball back in the direction you came with the sole of your foot. Then immediately continue going in the same direction with a quick dribble forward with the instep or inside of your foot. This change of pace makes the defender slow down for an instant and can create the opportunity to beat him. Remember, you know what you are going to do, and he doesn't, so he has to react to you. This is a great move to practice when you are just dribbling around the field to warm up.

As stated earlier, a soccer player needs a move to beat a defender to the right and left, as well as a move to change direction on the field with the ball. A change of direction move can be used when a player has trouble going past a quick defender and has to dribble laterally. It can also be used when the ball is on one side of the field with many defenders and a player needs to quickly switch it to the other side of the field to continue the attack.

The *reverse dribble* and *behind-the-leg* moves are two changes of direction moves similar to their basketball counterparts.

4. **Reverse dribble move.** Your players can use the reverse dribble move when they are moving toward a touchline from the middle of the field. Let's pretend your player has the ball in the center of midfield. As the defender challenges him, the dribbler starts to accelerate toward the right touchline with the ball. Once he gets the defender moving with him, he quickly moves between the ball and defender with his body and shields the ball. He immediately pivots and turns his back toward the defender and dribbles back in the direction that he just came from. To dribble the ball back in the opposite direction, the dribbler must bring his right foot up and curl the outside of his foot around the ball and pull or drag the ball back. A great way to set up this move is for the player to fake a pass or kick toward a player near the sideline just before pulling the ball back with the outside of his foot.

5. **Behind-the-leg move.** The behind-the-leg move is like the behind-the-back dribble in basketball. In soccer, let's pretend that the dribbler is once again moving laterally across the field to the right as the defender is challenging him. He starts to accelerate and gets the defender moving with him. He steps between the defender and the ball with his left foot to shield the ball. He immediately pivots while facing the defender and taps the ball behind his left leg in the direction he just came from. He taps the ball using the inside of his right foot (around the eyelets) to do this move. As with the reverse dribble move, a great way to set up this move is for the player to fake a pass or kick toward a player near the sideline just before tapping the ball back behind his leg.

6. **Sole back move.** The sole back move is another change of direction move that is one of the easier moves for young players to learn. This move can be made anywhere on the field. It is normally used in a situation where the dribbler is moving with the ball and can't seem to get free of a defender. Set up this move by dribbling faster and forcing the defender to pick up his pace to stay with you. As with other change-of-direction moves, make sure to keep your body between the ball and the defender when you do it. For exam-

ple, if you are moving to the right, start this move by stepping on the ground between the ball and the defender with your left foot. Next, lightly place the sole of your right foot on top of the ball and pull the ball back in the opposite direction that you were dribbling. Immediately continue going in that direction and accelerate away from the defender. When you are doing this move, the position of your body will be just like it is when you are shielding a ball from a defender. It is important to stress to the kids not to step down hard on the ball, otherwise they may trip over it. Have them pretend that it is a balloon and they have to step lightly on it or they will pop it.

The most important thing to teach your players about beating any defender is that the defender will remain "beaten" only for a moment. Too often an attacker will beat a defender and then casually dribble off, only to have the defender give immediate chase and steal the ball back. Then the attacker has to beat the same defender again. Whenever the attacker beats a defender, *he must accelerate quickly away from the opponent*.

Now that we know some moves, let's try them in a few drills.

1. **1v1 Dribble at your partner.** Partners each have a ball and face each other from 15 yards apart. One partner serves as the "captain" and tells his partner which move they are going to do and the direction they will each go. He says "go!" when both partners are ready to do a move. As they dribble directly toward each other, they will have to decide when to do the move. They are pretending that their partner is a defender and they have to avoid running into him. If they do the move too soon, they will not effectively beat their

partner (defender). If they do the move too late, they will lose the ball as it bounces into their partner. After doing the move and passing by their partner, the players continue to dribble so that they are 15 yards away, and then turn and face each other and wait to start again.

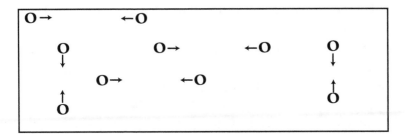

2. **Attack the Cone.** Cones should be set up approximately 15 yards away from one another. Every player has a ball and stands facing a cone about 2 yards away. The coach will give a move for the players to do. When he says "go," the players do the move at the cone (defender). After they pass by that cone, the players continue to a different cone and do the move again. Finally, they go to another cone and do the move and then dribble to a fourth cone and stop their ball 6 inches from the cone with their foot on top of it. Only one person may be at a cone. The last person standing with his foot on his ball at a cone has a letter. Then continue the same exercise with the same move, a different move, or a combination of moves. Once a player has two letters, she takes her cone with her and proceeds to "GO" to the side. This is a time that players can get some help practicing the move on their own.

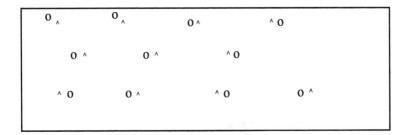

2V1 OFFENSIVE EXERCISES

When your players get a 2v1 situation going (two attackers and one defender), your team has achieved the ideal offensive situation: *NUMERICAL SUPERIORITY.* This allows your team to at least penetrate the opponent's defense and perhaps get a shot on goal.

For the first drill set up a 10-yard by 10-yard practice area. Have one player positioned as a defender and stand between two cones about 8 yards from the two attackers.

There are three pairs of attackers in two lines. The attackers alternate and the defender plays defense for three turns. One pair starts with the ball, and the player with the ball goes directly at the defender. Some youngsters think they will lose the ball to the defender, but *the attacker's attitude must be that they are in charge and the defender is in trouble.* As each player attacks, she must be thinking one of two things: (1) fake a pass to her teammate and dribble past the defender, or (2) fake dribbling the ball by the defender, drawing the defender's attention, and passing to her teammate.

The positioning of the receiving player is extremely important.

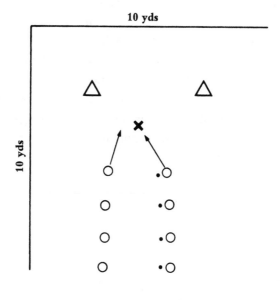

X—DEFENDER

She must try to stay a yard behind the attacker for three reasons: (1) if she runs too far ahead in the attacking third of the field, she may be offside; (2) if the receiver is at midfield, and not offside, another defender will probably be giving cover (support) and step up to intercept the pass (if you watch a soccer game, you will notice that 2v2 is the usual situation wherever the ball is); and (3) to avoid having the defender cut off the passing angle by stepping forward with her leg.

MISCELLANEOUS EXERCISES

1. **Wall pass—soccer's "Give and go."** In this 2v1 exercise, the passer plays the ball to the receiver and gets a return pass as he runs behind the defender.

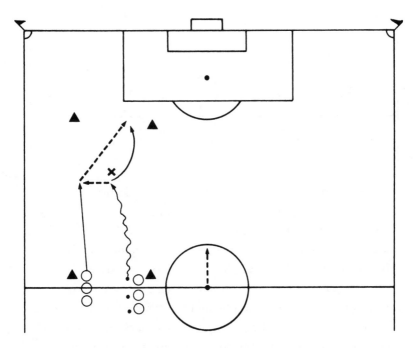

SOCCER'S VERSION OF BASKETBALL'S
"GIVE AND GO."

2. **Overlap.** In this situation, the player starts by passing the ball directly to the receiver. The passer then runs around the receiver, and

the receiver dribbles diagonally at the defender. The receiver keys the defender and either passes it back to the original passer or keeps the ball and dribbles past.

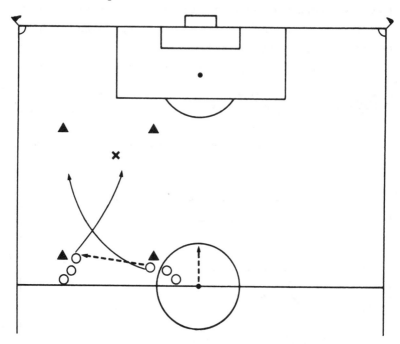

3. **Takeover.** Here the passer dribbles across in front of the defender as the receiver runs behind his teammate.

The ball is exchanged as the player with the ball leaves the ball for his teammate, using right foot to right foot or left foot to left foot. In this way, a collision is avoided. (See diagram on next page.)

4. **Diagonal.** Your team can also attack 2v1 by directing a receiver to make a diagonal run behind the defender. If the defender goes with the receiver, the passer continues unmolested. If the defender covers the passer, he passes to the receiver. The receiver must not allow the defender to stand in the passing lane between the passer and receiver.

Now you must develop these 2v1 tactics in a more gamelike situation. Achieve this with a simple exercise where your players attack two-on-one and finish with a shot on goal. Follow this exercise by adding another goal for the defender to counter the attack. Finally, have the kids play a small-sided game of 4v4 or 5v5 and give points every time a team successfully completes a 2v1.

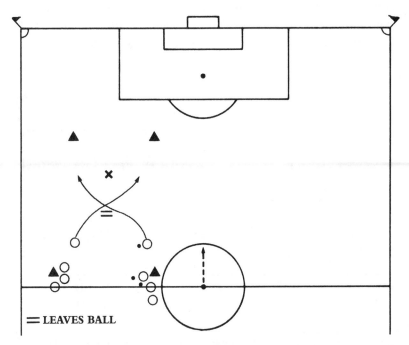

As mentioned before, the 2v2 situation is much closer to actual game conditions. So, practice the same exercises in the 2v2 configuration.

3V2 OFFENSIVE EXERCISES

A good exercise to create opportunities for 2v1 attacks is the 3v2 drill. Two players start on defense and stand on the 18-yard line. Three offensive players start about 20 yards inside the midfield line. One player starts with the ball in the center of the field, and two players start about 20 yards on each side of this player. The center player begins the exercise by passing the ball to the player on the right side (you can switch sides later). After passing the ball, the center player runs around the player on the right side and overlaps. This is the start of a 2v1 attack. The new player with the ball dribbles at the defender on his side and creates a 2v1 opportunity with the overlapping player. The dribbler must decide how to best attack. First, he can pass the ball to the overlapping player, who in turn can cross the ball to the other attackers for a header or shot on goal (Diagram A). Second, if he sees that the defender is moving toward the overlapping player to cover him, he can attack the other defender and either shoot the ball himself or pass it to the attacker who started on the left side (Diagram B). Keep rotating a new group of three attackers each time and switch defenders every three opportunities.

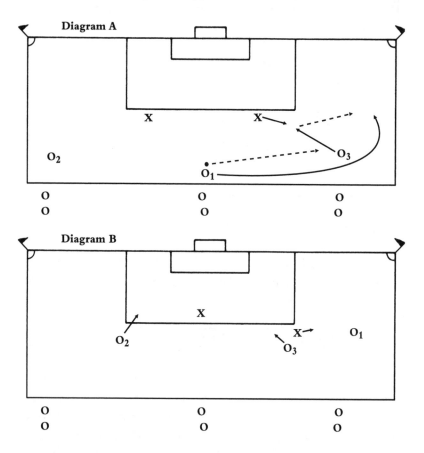

NUMBERS DOWN

In most of these exercises, your offense has played with numerical superiority, meaning you have more players on offense than you do on defense. While this does occur in soccer games, more often the defense outnumbers the offense during the course of play. So it is important to drill your offense in "numbers down" exercises, wherein you have more players on defense than you do on offense. For example, take your players to the offensive third of the field. Have three players attack four defenders and try to create a shot on goal. If they create a shot opportunity, even if they don't score, they start over again with the ball and try to create another scoring chance. If the defense steals the ball before a shot is taken, give the attackers a chance to try to steal the ball back. If the defense maintains possession for 10 seconds, then rotate in three new attackers. This exercise can also be played in 4v5, 5v6, or 6v7 situations.

Shadow Drill. The Shadow drill is a great team offensive drill that will help you see if your players know where they should go on the field regardless of where the ball might be. In this drill, start out with NO defenders. Put your entire team out on the field, plus one extra goalkeeper in the far goal. Start at the defensive end, give your goalkeeper the ball, and have him punt it down the field. Wait and see where the ball goes.

Once someone has possession of ball, have your team stop. Now, check and see where all of the players are. Did the defenders push up? Are they supporting the ball along with the midfielders? Are the forwards moving into a position where they can receive a pass and go on the attack? Did the goalkeeper move up to support the defenders?

Next, have the player with the ball pass it to someone else and then stop your team again. Check to see if the passer passed the ball to the correct person. Was there someone who had a better opportunity to receive the ball and possibly score that he should have passed to instead? Continue passing the ball around the field and stop occasionally to point out if the players are in the right position and if they passed the ball to the correct person. Once you get to the goal, let the team take a shot at the goalkeeper. After the shot, have that goalkeeper punt the ball out. Once your team controls the ball, have them pass the ball back toward their goal until their goalkeeper receives it. Then start the drill again.

A variation of this drill is to add some defenders in front of the goal you are attacking. Start the drill the same way, but now have your team challenge to score once they are in the attacking third.

OFFENSIVE TEAM DRILLS

So now you have some drills to develop individual skills and basic offensive tactics. But what do you do to develop team tactics in practice using all of your players? Here are a few drills to get you started.

1. **Four goal drill #1.** Break up your squad into two teams—one with pinnies and one without. Using cones, set up two goals 5 yards inside the touch line on each side of the field. The cones should be about 5 yards apart and should be about 25 yards away from each other and in a straight line. One team will attack the two goals on one side of the field and the other team will attack the goals on the other side of the field.

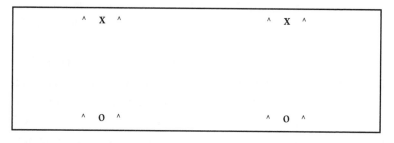

The drill begins with both teams in the middle of the field between the goals with one ball. The object of the game is to learn to play with your head up and change the direction of attack if there are defenders in the way. The only way a goal can be scored is by passing the ball through one of the goals that your team is attacking from either direction. The goal is counted if a teammate receives the ball under control on the other side of the goal.

As your team starts to attack a goal, defenders will run in front of that goal to prevent a goal from being scored. The attacking players must keep their heads up to see which goal has the most defenders in front of it. After they see which goal has the fewest players defending, that team should immediately attack that goal. Before a pass is even made out toward that goal, some players should already be near the goal. Coaches should point out players who are nearer the other goal and credit them for doing something positive. As a result of not running toward the teammate with the ball and becoming part of the "beehive" effect, they were able to receive a pass with fewer defenders around and had a better chance to score at the other goal.

During this drill, it is important for the coaches to continue to ask the team with the ball, "Do you really want to attack that goal? And do they have too many players in front of that goal?" Players without the ball will learn the valuable lesson that they should look in front of a goal and see which goal has too many defenders. Once that is determined, they can move toward the other goal and call for a pass.

This is a great time to point out the importance of staying away from the ball unless the player is involved in the immediate attack, e.g., 1v1, 2v1. Now is the time to point out that if a player without the ball keeps his distance from the ball (and doesn't bunch up), defenders will have to run farther to defend him, and he will have more time to control the ball, pass, dribble, or shoot it.

2. **Four Goal Drill #2.** This is a good variation of drill #1. The only difference is that the goals are placed differently. The goals that one team attacks are placed facing each other, 5 yards inside the touch line. The goals for the second team also face each other, the same distance apart as the first goals but in the middle third of a soccer field. One team attacks both "O" goals, and the other team attacks the "X" goals.

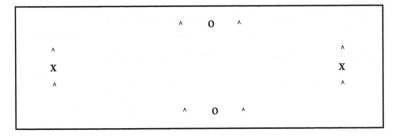

3. **Captain's Soccer.** This is a great drill to help kids learn to get free to receive the ball and to play with their heads up and look for

open teammates. Divide your team in half, using pinnies to distinguish players by color. One team starts on offense, the other on defense. They switch back and forth as their team maintains or loses possession of the ball. Both teams designate one player to be their captain.

The captain's job is to get free from defenders and receive the ball under control from a teammate. The captain's team receives a point every time he receives the ball in this manner.

The captain should move away from the ball and take defenders with him as he looks for open spaces. Once he sees a teammate is ready to pass the ball, he should run away from the defenders into a space to receive a pass. If he controls the pass, his team receives one point.

Once the captain is able to get free and receive a pass, he may be able to immediately pass the ball back to a teammate and receive a second pass for another point. He should continue passing back and forth with his teammates as often as possible and get as many points as he can before he is defended again and not free to receive a pass.

If the defense succeeds in stealing the ball, they go on offense and attempt to pass to their captain to score points. The defense may decide that the easiest way to stop the captain from receiving the ball is to have everyone defend him. That creates another scoring opportunity with a different tactic. A team may also score a point by making five passes in a row of at least 5 yards to anyone else on their team. It's a good idea to tell the kids that two players cannot make all five passes in a row. This stops two players from running into a corner of the field and just passing the ball back and forth quickly.

After a few minutes, change captains and start keeping score all over again to see which team scores the most points.

11
DEFENSIVE
TACTICS

As we said earlier, soccer is a game of opposites. While attackers try to stretch the defense, the defense condenses itself to defend the most dangerous area, which is in front of the goal. (At higher levels of play, players will learn to defend areas all over the field as they *become* dangerous. Your defensive goal area is not very dangerous if your opponents have the ball 10 yards in front of their goal.) Attackers will try to get more players in an area than there are defenders, while defenders will of course try to outnumber the attackers. When the opposing team has penetrated your defensive third of the field, they will try to be creative and improvise. Your defenders should try to cut off play options for the attackers. This will make the attackers' moves more predictable and easier to handle.

Assume that you have just assigned a youngster to play left back. It's the first time he has played this position. Apprehensive, he asks what he should do. Calmly tell him to mark the right wing. Identify that player and explain that he should first stay between the wing and the goal (goalside). Make certain he plays far enough away from the wing so if a ball is kicked over his head toward the goal, he won't be outraced to the ball. If his opponent does make a long kick, all your player should do is pass the ball back to the goalkeeper or turn away with the ball. The goalkeeper will tell him what should be done. Whatever he does, he must play the ball the way he is facing. He should not turn back into the chasing player. The ball can be stolen easily and may lead to a goal.

If his opponent passes the ball on the ground to the wing, your back should run forward and try to *beat the wing to the ball*. Remember, as your back gets closer to the wing, he must be more under control. If he approaches the wing out of control, he may crash into him and be called for a foul. If the wing gets the ball before your back, he may use the back's speed and aggressiveness against him and fake by him. If the wing beats your back to the ball, stress to the back *not to let the wing turn with the ball*. He cannot pass the ball forward or take a shot if your back does not allow him to turn. The wing will be forced to pass the ball back in the direction of his own goal. This will give the other defenders time to get back on defense. The back should try to poke the ball away from the wing when he is behind him.

Let's pretend that the wing was able to turn with the ball. Maybe the back slipped. Now the wing faces your back and begins to attack. If the back plays in front of the wing, he can beat him to the left, right, or through the legs. He is at the wing's mercy because he has no idea which way he will attack. The back should try to force the wing in one direction—to the sideline. To do this he just has to move to the inside of the field. This accomplishes a number of things: the wing can only move in one direction—to the outside; as the wing dribbles down the field, his shooting angle becomes worse and he has less chance to score; with the ball at the sideline, and not the middle, other defenders have a much easier task marking their men. They can slide toward the ball and create a defensive triangle between the ball, their opponent, and themselves. Since the ball can be passed in only one direction, your players won't be deceived, and with proper positioning can handle the pass safely.

Forwards must learn to play defense: If a forward loses the ball on attacks, she must be the first person back on defense.

As the forwards chase the ball from behind, midfielders run back to get between the goal and their opponents. Everyone marks an opponent. To give your defense time to prepare, the player who pressures the ball should delay the attack by *jockeying* his opponent. (Jockeying is a delaying tactic that results from a player "bothering" the man with the ball, forcing him to slow down and/or move to one side or another.) His teammates now have time to get back on defense and mark their men. Defenders must pick up the most dangerous man first. It's usually obvious who that is. If one attacking player is 40 yards from the goal and another attacker is 20 yards away, guess who's more dangerous! Make this point very clear to your players.

ZONE VS. MAN-TO-MAN DEFENSES

Coaches must determine which type of defensive system of play to use based upon the abilities and strengths of their players. They may choose to play a zone defense where players are responsible for an area on the field, man-to-man where the defensive player is responsible for a specific player, or a combination of the two systems.

Regardless of the system of play, there are certain defensive concepts that must be followed:

1. The defender must stay between his opponent and the goal. If a defender simply does this, he will at least have an opportunity to defend his opponent if he attacks with, or without, the ball.

2. When marking an offensive player who does not have the ball, the defender must move (slough) toward the ball. This is called creating a **defensive triangle**. Creating a defensive triangle puts the defender in a position that is defensively sound.

By sloughing toward the ball, the defender has a head start toward beating his opponent to the ball when the ball is passed or shot and rebounds in his direction.

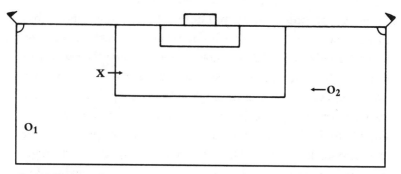

O₁—Offensive player
O₂—Offensive player passing or shooting the ball
X—Defender

By sloughing toward the ball, the defender can also help his teammate who is defending the person with the ball should he be beaten by the attacker.

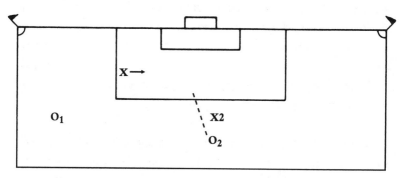

O₁—Offensive player
O₂—Offensive player beating the defender
X—Defender
X2—Defender being beaten by the attacker with the ball

In both cases, if the defender did not slough toward the ball, he could be beaten to the goal by the person he is marking. He would also not be able to help a teammate who is beaten by an attacker with the ball.

Following these defensive concepts is much simpler if you are playing man to man. However, more experienced opponents will try to move all over the field, seeking to draw defenders away with them.

By doing this, they hope to create openings for attackers to beat defenders and not have defensive help.

When playing zone defense, the concepts remain the same; however, players defend their area first and must be alert to help in a bordering zone if a teammate is beaten. Sometimes teams will try to put more than one attacker into a zone to create "numerical superiority." When this happens, a nearby defender without an attacker in his zone must be ready to slide over to help. Communication is a key in this situation; when a defender sees that there are two attackers in his zone, he must yell out to let his teammates know.

EXERCISES TO DEVELOP DEFENSE

1. **1v1 five-second drill.** Divide your team, lining up half of the players 40 yards from the goal, each player with a ball. The other half of the team acts as defenders, lined up on one side of a goalpost. The exercise begins when the first defender runs out from the goal. When the first player in the attacking line sees the defender run, he begins to attack 1v1, and the attacker has five seconds to score. The defender should force the attacker to one side and not allow him to turn back.

2. **Can't-turn drill.** Set up two grids, 10 yards by 20 yards, side by side. Split the team in half so that each group may do the same exercise in one grid. Two players are in the center of the grid, and two players—passers—stand at each end of the grid with two balls each.

The object of the exercise is for one player in the grid to receive a ball, turn with it, and pass the ball to the player on the other side. The defensive objective is to beat the offensive player to the ball. If the defender can't beat him to the ball, he does not allow him to turn. The offensive player can pass the ball back the way he is facing and try to get free again. If the defender steals the ball or knocks it out of the grid, he becomes the new offensive player as the players switch roles. Limit the time to about 30 to 45 seconds. After the players have had a few opportunities, combine both groups and do the same exercise with 2v2 in the entire grid area. This exercise will help

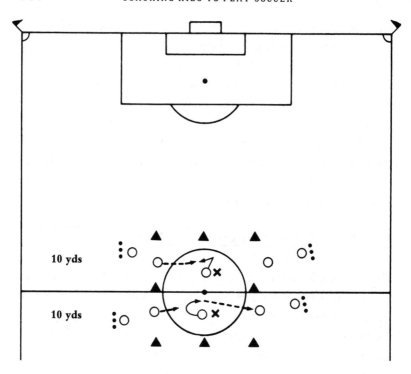

develop the player's ability to give cover and create a defensive triangle when not pressuring the ball.

3. **3v3 midfield drill.** This is a very important TEAM defensive drill. It stresses maintaining a defensive triangle and helps teach players to focus on seeing both *the man* they are defending and *the ball* at all times.

Set up your team in three lines at midfield with a center forward, right wing, and left wing positioned with defenders marking each player. *In this drill, defenders are not allowed to steal the ball.* They can only change their defensive positions on the field. The defenders move from pressuring the ball when the person they are marking has it, to supporting their teammate at a 45-degree angle, to covering for both teammates when the ball is on the far side of the field.

The drill begins with the middle defender marking the center forward and pressuring the ball (he cannot steal it!). The outside defenders, who are marking the wings, move inside at a 45-degree an-

gle to practice supporting the middle defender as they would in a
game in the event he was beaten by the center forward. Of course
that is not allowed in this drill!

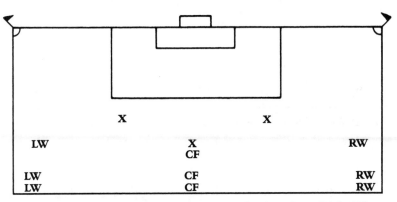

X—Defense   CF—Center Forward   LW—Left Wing   RW—Right Wing

The center forward passes the ball to a wing and moves slightly
toward him for support. When the right wing receives the ball, the
left outside defender pressures the ball without stealing it. The middle defender moves back at a 45-degree angle to the left outside defender to practice supporting the left defender as they would in a
game in the event he was beaten by the right wing. The right outside
defender moves farther back toward the center of the field and creates a diagonal line of defenders with the middle defender and
left outside defender. He becomes the supporting defender. Defenders should never be in a straight line across the field as once a person is beaten there will be no other defenders to help pick up the
attacker.

X—Defense   CF—Center Forward   LW—Left Wing   RW—Right Wing

The drill continues with the right wing passing the ball back to the center forward and the defenders adjusting their positions as well. Next, the center forward passes to the left wing and the defenders adjust their defensive positions in the opposite way. The drill continues back and forth until the players reach the goal. At that time, the offensive players jog back and become the new defenders and the defenders go to the end of the offensive lines.

12
RESTARTS

During a game, the referee may stop play for a number of reasons. The act of putting the ball back into play is called a *restart*. Because restarts are so important to the game, this entire chapter deals with them.

Restarts. Restarts (free kicks, corner kicks, throw-ins) are very dangerous situations and must have everyone's undivided attention, especially the goalkeeper's. When your team is setting up its defensive wall, the goalie must yell out the number of people needed. A defensive wall is just what it sounds like: a wall of stationary players designed to present an obstacle to the opposing player taking a free kick. The wall is required to be at least 10 yards from the ball.

If your opposition is out of range and not attempting a shot, there is no reason to have a wall. Once the goalkeeper calls for the number of players he wants in the wall, set it up first by lining up the tallest player with the near post. The goalkeeper should not line up the ball, as a shot may be taken while he is occupied. Let a midfielder do it. If the opposition is taking a corner kick, get two players, one on each post, to cover the goal in the event the goalie must come out of the goal to catch the ball. Don't put a back on the post. Coaches do this all the time. Isn't it silly to have your best defenders guard a post and your worst defenders, the forwards, guard the opposition's best players?

If the opposition has a throw-in in your defensive third of the field, they may have a player who can reach the goal. Remember: the ball cannot be thrown into the goal. It must touch someone, goal-keepers included, before it can count as a goal. Don't forget that the offensive team can't be offside when the ball is thrown in.

Of course, the main advantage goalkeepers maintain over field players is that they can use their hands, but remember that this advantage exists only in the penalty area.

Throw-in. When the ball goes over the touch line (sideline), the team that touched it last loses possession. The other team now throws the ball back into play. The player throwing the ball must toss with two hands (forming a "W" with thumbs and index finger). Players cannot throw the ball directly into the goal; it must touch someone else first. Remember, the offensive team can't be offside on a throw-in.

THROW-INS

When the ball passes the sideline (touchline), the team that did not touch it last is awarded the throw-in from the spot the ball went out of bounds. Throw-ins must be practiced in order to prevent illegal throw-ins, which results in the other team getting the ball. Here are the rules for teaching the throw-in:

1. The thrower must hold the ball and throw it with two hands. Form a "W" behind the ball with your hands.

2. The ball must start from behind the head and be released over the head.

3. Both feet must remain on the ground during the throw.

4. The body must face in the direction of the throw.

One of the things you should try to encourage your players to do is take the throw-in as quickly as possible when you have an opportunity to attack. Quite often your opponent is spread out over the field and not in good defensive position when the ball goes out of bounds. It is often possible to immediately pick up the ball and throw it in to the teammate who is running into an open space on attack. (Their run should usually be forward to a space where they can control the ball and continue with the attack.)

THROW-IN EXERCISES

In soccer the sideline is called the touchline. This is a good way to remind your young players the only time they can "touch" the ball with their hands is when it goes over the touchline. When it does go over the touchline, it is thrown back into play with a throw-in.

You have now learned the rules and how to execute a legal throw-in. Here is how to practice it with your team.

1. **Throw and Catch.** Working with a partner, have your players stand 10 yards apart (closer if your team has difficulty reaching their

partner) and throw the soccer ball back and forth like you would when warming up before a baseball or softball game, but using a throw-in technique.

As players take throw-ins back and forth to one another, challenge them to throw the ball to their partners at different body heights: head high, chest high, at the feet. This will give them practice throwing the ball to different body parts and will give options to their teammates when they receive the ball.

Now, you should be loosened up and ready for some more challenging throw-in drills.

2. Hit the Spot. One partner takes a throw-in to her partner and tells her that she is going to throw it to her head first, then her chest, and then her foot. Remind your players that this is a pass that they want their teammates to be able to pass back to them under control. They are not playing dodgeball, so the throw-in should not knock their teammates out! The partner heads the ball back to the person who took the throw-in. The next throw-in is aimed at the person's chest. The receiver redirects the ball to a side, controls the ball, and passes it back with her foot.

The next throw-in is at the person's foot and is passed back with one touch to the partner who took the throw-in. Now the partners switch and go in the same body order. Once the players have success, you do not have to tell them where the ball is being thrown.

3. **Throw-in Dodge.** This is a lot of fun and also gives you an opportunity to see if your players are using legal throw-ins.

Divide your team into #1s, #2s, and #3s. Set up a grid area approximately 20 yards square (adjust the size according to the number of players and their size for safety). Use part of the penalty area lines and cones to set up this grid. Use the four or five softest soccer balls you have, or even indoor balls if softer.

Once you set up the grid area, have the #1s spread out in the grid area. The #2s and #3s surround the grid area holding the soccer balls. The object of the game is for the #1s to dodge the throw-ins and try to be the last person remaining. The #2s and #3s must throw in the ball using a legal throw-in and try to hit the #1s to eliminate them. The important rule to stress is that the ball cannot hit a player

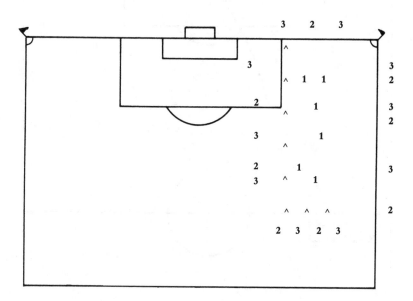

until it has hit the ground *at least* one time. If a rolling ball hits a player, the player is also out.

If the ball hits a player on the fly, the player stays in the game *and* the person who threw in the ball has to do five push-ups or five sit-ups or a lap—you decide. The players throwing the balls can only hold the ball for 5 seconds. Sometimes the ball may stop inside the grid. The players inside the grid must tap the ball to the players outside the grid, but they are still targets at this time.

Once only one player remains, the #2s go in the grid and try to be the last one remaining. Once that occurs, the #3s go in until the end of the game. Let the three teams have one more chance to go in and try to be the last person remaining on their team. After every team has had a second chance, have all of the winners from each of the rounds go into the grid. The winner of this round is the champ. Make sure you have a little prize ready for the winner—M&Ms work very well!

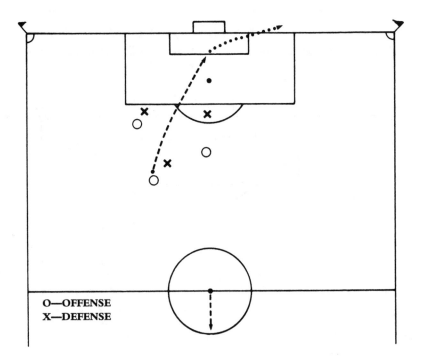

O—OFFENSE
X—DEFENSE

Goal kick. If an offensive player touches the ball before it goes over the goal line, the defensive team is awarded a goal kick. Anyone on the defending team can take the goal kick as long as it's taken from on the ground. You can't pick it up and punt it! If your goalkeeper is capable of taking an acceptable goal kick that can carry a safe distance from the goal, let him. This will allow your other players to move up the field and keep defenders farther away from the goal. You may even get an offside call against your opponents if they do not move back with your defenders.

Make sure that whoever is taking the goal kick tees the ball up on the ground. Don't let him just roll it somewhere in the goal area and kick it from where it stops. Where do you think the ball will stop rolling? On a high spot, level ground, or in a small hole? Probably in a hole!

The kick must be taken from anywhere within half of the 6-yard goal area on the side of the goal line that the ball went over. No one may touch the ball after a goal kick until it has gone completely outside the penalty area.

Make sure to have your player kick the ball to the side of the field that you are taking the goal kick from. Never kick the ball across the field. It is also important to understand that just because you have the ball, you really aren't on offense. Once you kick the ball in the air away from your goal, the other team has a fifty-fifty chance to get possession. So make sure that your player, and especially your defenders, are near the player they have to mark in the event you lose possession of the ball after the goal kick.

Corner kick. If the ball was last touched by a defender before going over the goal line, a corner kick is awarded to the offensive team. The corner kick is taken from inside the corner arc on the side of the field where the ball crossed over the goal line.

Corner kicks are great opportunities to score goals, especially if you have a player who can reach the goal with a corner kick and players who are able to head the ball on goal. If you do have a player with a strong leg, have your players run to spots in front of the goal where they have a good chance to score when the ball arrives:

a. even with the near post about 6 yards away from the goal line (1)

b. in the center of the goal area just inside the penalty spot— about 10 yards from the goal (2)

c. 4 yards outside the far post and 8 yards from the goal line (3)

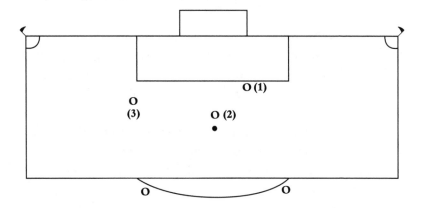

It is also a geat idea to have two players stand on both sides of the penalty arc (D) where it intersects with the penalty area. Many times balls are headed, kicked, or rebound away from the front of the goal area toward the penalty area, and there is a great opportunity for players to kick the ball at the goal as the goalkeeper may be screened.

If you have some taller players on your team who head the ball well, you may want to play some high balls in front of the goal. If your players are smaller, hard, low-driven passes may work better, as your players can use their quickness and agility to get to the ball before their opponent. This type of pass is often deflected to teammates and may lead to confusion in front of the goal. Some teams also put a player in front of the goalkeeper and have them run to the ball to try to head it either in the goal or back to a teammate. They actually pretend to be an "attacking goalkeeper."

Short corner. A short corner is an offensive opportunity using two players to create a shot at the goal. It is usually attempted by a team who is playing on a wide field and does not have a player who can reach the goal or if their team does not have very good headers and they are continually beaten to the high balls by their opponent.

All defensive players must stand at least 10 yards away from the ball for a corner kick; however, offensive players may stand as close as they like. The easiest short corner is to have two players stand side by side in the corner arc. One player passes the ball to a teammate and then runs toward the goal (overlap). The two offensive players attack 2v1 against the first defender that approaches them. If the ball is passed to the overlapping player, he can shoot. The player with the ball may choose to continue dribbling the ball along the goal line and then cross the ball to one of the three dangerous spots previously mentioned.

Another version of the short corner is to have a player run from in front of the goal toward a teammate who is taking the corner kick. The defender marking this running player must stop 10 yards before the ball. This allows the player in the corner arc to pass the ball to the player running toward him and then receive a pass back. The corner kicker then has a moving ball coming toward him (like in kick ball) and will find it much easier to kick the ball farther and perhaps reach the front of the goal.

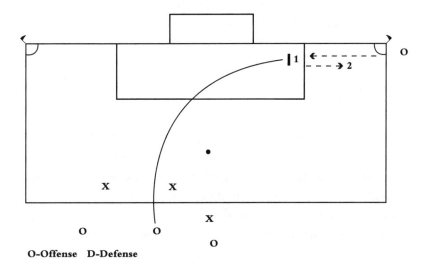

O-Offense D-Defense

Defending the corner kick. There are various ways to defend corner kicks. Some teams will play man-to-man and match up their better defenders with the better attackers. They may also match up defenders with attackers by height or speed. Other teams may defend with a zone and have each player be responsible for an area. Some teams may also use a combination of these systems. Regardless of the defensive setup you use for a corner kick, put one player on each post to help defend the goal in the event the goalkeeper must come out to make a save and does not get the ball. *Please* don't assign your defenders to cover the goalposts! So many coaches do that. Does it make sense to ask your best defenders, who have been covering the best offensive players throughout the game, to now stand by a goalpost while other weaker defenders are marking the best offensive players on the other team? We don't think so. Put your forwards on the goalposts. They probably have the most skill and may be able to head the ball away and save a goal or juggle the ball away from the goal. Keep your best players marking the players they have been marking (as long as they are doing a good job).

If you are playing a zone system, position four players along the 6-yard line. They shoud be your better headers and defenders. Put three more players about 10 yards away from the goal on each side of the penalty spot and inside it as well. You have already put two players on the goalposts, so that leaves one more player to stand in front of the person taking the corner kick. Remember, he must be 10 yards away. The person facing the corner kicker is an important player, as he will come out if your opponent tries to play a short corner. The closest person inside the penalty spot on the side of the ball will also come over to cover a short corner.

You may also decide to defend the corner kick by playing both man-to-man and zone. In this case, you may play some of your players in a zone and also mark the one or two best opponents man-to-man. If you decide to do that, take players from one or two of the defensive positions that are inside the penalty spot from the goal. Once you decide which defenders will play man-to-man, you will need to reevaluate where you place certain players. Regardless of the

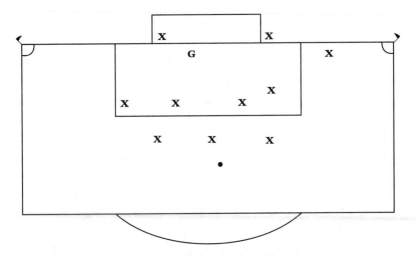

system you use, you will have to decide what your players can and cannot do, and then decide what system works best for them.

Free kick. There are two kinds of free kicks—direct and indirect. (These break down into restarts in shooting distance and out-of-shooting distance, but you should consult the rules section to see what foul results in what kick.) When the opposing team is within shooting distance, set up your defense in a wall to block the part of the goal the goalkeeper leaves empty while he plays the opponent's direct kick. Your goalkeeper must handle balls kicked around or over the wall. The offense will try to put the ball in play immediately before a wall can be set up. The kicking player will either take a shot on goal (direct) or pass to a teammate for a shot (indirect).

Your goalkeeper should call out the number of players needed in the wall, and a field player should line everyone up with the near post. When your team has set the wall, the player who lined it up should mark any unmarked player. If everyone is marked, he should give chase to any ball passed for a shot or overlap. Keep your backs out of the wall, if possible. Usually they are your best defenders and will be more effective marking players. If your opponent is out of shooting distance, he may try to chip the ball in front of the goal. In this situation defensive players should mark a man and hold at the

18-yard line; any ball chipped into the goal area can be handled by the goalkeeper as the defenders cover the attacking players. Defenders must stay with their men until the ball is safely in the goalkeeper's hands.

When your team gets a free kick, use the strengths of individual players to determine what you want to try. Do you have one or two swift players who can outrace their men to a spot in front of the goal? Do you have a good passer who can chip over defenders to that spot? Do you have a player who is able to bend balls over or around a wall? Don't be afraid to be a little deceptive—designing these "set pieces" in practice will make for more productive free kicks in games.

Penalty kick. Penalty kicks are high-percentage shots and should be as automatic as an extra point in football. The penalty spot is 12 yards away from the goal. During the kick the goalkeeper must stay on the goal line but can move along the line until the ball is played. Everyone except the shooter must be out of the penalty area and penalty

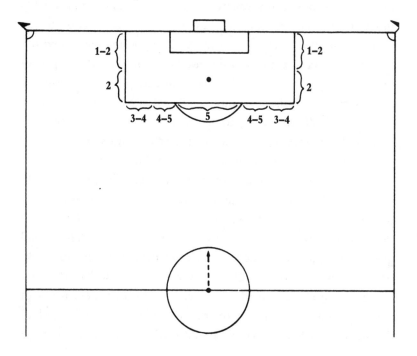

arc (D). The shooter chooses a side and tries to place the ball within 3 feet of that post. Many players will take a penalty kick using a push pass. Done with the inside of the foot, this shot is more accurate than an instep kick and can still be struck powerfully enough to beat the goalkeeper. At higher levels of play, goalkeepers will guess the side the player is shooting for and dive in that direction. At the youth level it is probably more realistic for the goalie to wait until the ball is shot and then react.

13

SYSTEMS OF PLAY (Where Do I Play, Coach?)

Regardless of where a youngster plays, he must understand that when his team has the ball he is on offense, and when the opponent has the ball he is on defense.

A team does not win or lose because it plays a particular system. The skill with which individual players and the team as a whole execute specific techniques and tactics determines who plays well and usually wins . . . or who plays less well and usually loses. Outstanding technique will make any system a successful one.

Before choosing a system for your team, analyze your players. What are their strengths and weaknesses? After careful consideration, determine who should play where so that everyone is matched to the most appropriate or practical position. Then choose a system.

Most team systems start with a minimum of four backs (plus goalkeeper), two midfielders, and two forwards. That leaves two players. Adding these to the backfield would weigh down your defense. Placing both of them as forwards would make you strong offensively, but too weak at midfield. Are the two midfielders strong enough to cover midfield by themselves? It might be wise to start out with three midfielders and three forwards until you really know your players. In this 4-3-3 system (always number from the back forward), you must have a back who reads the game very well, is a good header, and has good skills. You may want to play him as a SWEEPER—a free back who doesn't have to mark anyone. The three remaining backs will mark your opponent's center forward and two wings. If you have a skilled, attack-oriented player at midfield, you should play him as an attacking midfielder and leave the other midfielders to cover for him and play more defensively. Do you have a forward who can beat defenders 1v1 and can cross a ball well? Perhaps he can play as a wing. Make sure to have him play on the side of your opponent's weakest back, once you determine who it is. This will create a mismatch to your advantage.

Here are a few diagrams to help you picture the various systems of play:

4-3-3- SYSTEM

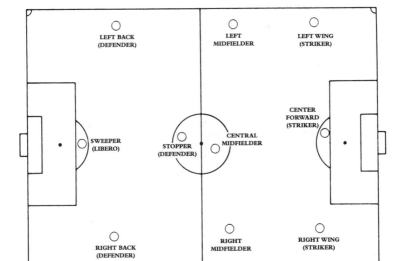

4-4-2 SYSTEM

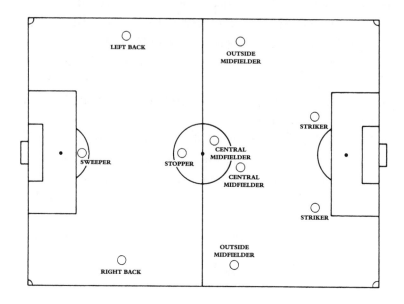

4-2-4 SYSTEM

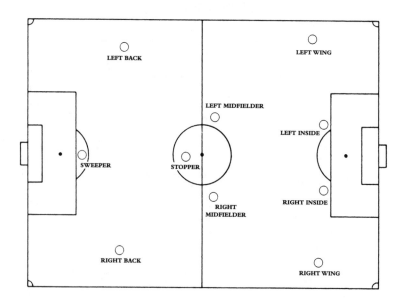

14
PREGAME
CHECK LIST

Before the practice or game ever begins, it is important to make sure you have everything necessary for your team to be successful. Using our pregame check list will help you remember to bring the things needed for practice, but this doesn't mean that *you* have to bring everything. If you have an assistant or two, they can help; parents are often happy to bring what they can. Check the medical kit beforehand to make certain you have sufficient supplies—bandages, gauze pads, Ace bandages, etc.

(You might want to remove this list from the book or copy it and attach it to your clipboard.)

OUR PREGAME CHECK LIST
1. Soccer Balls
2. Cones, corner flags
3. Score book—with clipboard and two pencils
4. Pinnies—or different-colored shirts—in case the other team shows up with the same uniform

5. Medical Kit—with emergency phone number(s)

6. Cell phones—make certain to have three individuals with working cell phones in the event of an emergency

6. Shin guards—two extra pairs for the kids who forget them

7. Cooler filled with bags of ice, unless you have instant ice packs

8. Rule book

9. Horn or whistle for substitutions

10. Roster of your players, their parents or guardians, and phone numbers

11. Directions to the field—expect a last-minute call from a parent who wants to come to the game and doesn't know how to get there or is lost

15

PRACTICE AND PREGAME WARM-UP ROUTINE

Before any practice or game you must warm up your players and stretch their playing muscles. Stretching will help prevent injuries and improve flexibility. Concentrate on the muscles specifically used often in soccer. Each player should stretch until it feels a bit un-comfortable, then hold back slightly. The stretch should be held for about eight seconds. No bouncing—just hold the stretch.

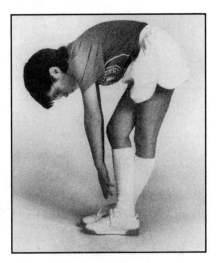

Stretching the Hamstrings (back of leg): Bend over at the waist with crossed legs and touch the toes.

Back Stretch: With legs apart, look as far over one shoulder as you can. Then twist the body in that direction and hold for eight seconds.

Quadriceps Stretch (front of thigh): Stand on one leg and pull the other foot behind as the knee is bent. Focus the eyes on a blade of grass or an object on the ground to help maintain balance, or just lean on a friend. Press the hip of the bent leg slightly forward.

Groin: Stretch sitting down and place the soles of the feet together with knees to the sides. Lean forward and try to press down lightly on the knees.

Be aware that each youngster is different and that some players will be more flexible than others. Explain to the youngsters that if they do not feel sufficiently warmed up at the end of the warm-up period, they may go ahead and continue to stretch some more. Spend extra time stretching muscle groups you plan to stress during practice. If you're going to concentrate on shooting, for example, do extra stretching for legs and back.

After light stretching, each player should do some running. Be sure to lead the players through all the types of running they will use in a game—forward, backward, sideways, shuffling sideways. Finish by hopping and then jumping to head an imaginary ball. After this type of running, do exercises *to increase circulation and body temperature* to warm up the muscles: sit-ups, push-ups, jumping jacks.

These exercises also improve the players' strength and fitness. Vary the exercises and the number of exercises and, whenever possible, use a ball when warming up to avoid boredom and promote enthusiasm. The more familiar a player is with the ball, the more relaxed he will be with it. Besides, it's more fun!

As important as the warm-up is the cool-down, which helps minimize muscle soreness. The cool-down aids circulation and clears waste products from the muscles. Light stretching again will help the cool-down process and help prevent the tightening of muscles that usually results from vigorous exercise.

Prior to a game, it is also important to warm up and stretch, but it is not necessary to try to build strength before a game by doing push-ups or sit-ups. Instead, pair the kids up. Have them warm up with a partner and a ball, using all the techniques they will use in the game. Have them imagine certain game situations and act them out—shooting at their partner as if he were the goal, taking goal kicks, heading the ball, taking corner kicks. Adding a third player to your warm-up can make it more creative. Then bring the team together and practice some tactics, both offensive and defensive. Try a 3v2 on goal. After this exercise, let your team do a few shooting drills. When the whistle blows, you are ready.

16

PREGAME, HALFTIME, AND POSTGAME TALKS

Okay, coach, so now you are ready to send your team onto the field for their first game. They are nervous and have butterflies in their stomachs—just like you! Let them know that it's normal to be a little nervous. In fact, if they weren't a little nervous *that* wouldn't be normal, and you would be worried. Tell them that they should act like they are little ducks paddling on the lake. On the surface, the ducks are nice and calm and gliding over the water. Underneath the water, however, they are paddling like crazy! Let them know that once the game starts, they will be fine.

It's important to remind them that they should be going out to play with a lot of confidence. They should all know there is nothing the other team can do that they aren't prepared for and won't be able to overcome. Let them know that the only way you could be disappointed in them is if they get out-hustled. So they need to play hard, fairly, and with good sportsmanship, and never give up.

During the pregame warm-up, try to speak with each of the players individually to remind them of what they need to do to play their best. You should try to think of their specific weaknesses and tell them to focus on the things you know they should be doing to be successful. You might say something to the player who stays too close to the attacker he is marking. Don't slough enough to the ball so he can help out on defense. This will also give him a head start to stay with his man if the ball is passed to him. Mention to the defender who just plays kickball that he must control the ball and pass it to a teammate unless it's in front of his goal. Mention to the goalkeeper to first look to throw the ball to a teammate on the opposite side from where the shot was taken after he makes a save.

Just before the game, give the entire team two things to focus on for the first half—one offensive thing and one defensive thing. More than that will be too much for them to concentrate on doing. On offense, focus on things like starting the game with everyone playing two- or three-touch and moving the ball around to get everyone on the team involved. Or after making two or three touches on one side of the field, switch the ball to the other side of the field. On defense, have them focus on beating their man to the ball when it is passed to them, and if he gets it, don't let him turn. Another focus point could be to remind the kids to slough to the ball when it is on the opposite side as the opponent may try to cross it to a teammate. You need to stress whatever you think are the keys to winning the game on offense and defense.

At halftime, you may have to make adjustments to these focus points. Try to determine how your opponent is hurting you offensively and defensively. Is there a very strong player on the other team? Perhaps you have to put one of your quick defenders on him all over the field and make someone else on their team beat you. Do they have a fast or skilled forward on the side of your weakest and slowest defender? Perhaps you have to switch the side your defenders are playing on, although hopefully you already made that change during the first half! You may find that some of your forwards (strikers) were tentative when they got close to the goal and were afraid to shoot. Sometimes when young players get close to the goal they will pass the ball instead of shooting it. When you have an opportunity, ask the tentative shooter what he was doing when he was close to the goal.

He will tell you that he passed the ball to a teammate. You should reply that he didn't pass the ball, he passed the responsibility. Let him know that when he is close enough to the goal and has an opportunity to shoot, he has an obligation to shoot! If he doesn't, the team misses a great opportunity to score that it will never get again.

As you continue to evaluate the first half, you may find that the other team is much quicker than your team. When the ball is just kicked by either team, they seem to get it most of the time. Well, that is why we work on our passing and receiving skills in practice! Have the kids "slow down to play faster." Instead of rushing their passes or kicking the ball when they are under pressure, remind them that they are the "King" (like in the King Drill) when they have the ball, and they should only pass when they are ready—just like in practice.

Also at halftime, reevaluate your offensive and defensive focus points. Should you keep them the same or focus on something more important in the second half? Let the kids know what they need to do on offense and defense—one of each—and send them out to play.

When the game is finished, in most cases you will be filled with great elation, or possibly some sorrow. Regardless, get the team to huddle up on the side of the field immediately. Be positive. Tell them they gave a great effort and you are proud of them. If you noticed any problems with, or between, any players, make sure to calm them down and stay next to them. Then have the kids line up to shake hands (or give a high five) with their opponents, congratulate them on a good game, and wish them luck the rest of the year. Don't forget to thank the opposing coaches and referees as well.

After congratulating the other team, bring your team together on the field away from spectators, and again be positive. Let them know that you are proud of them, point out some wonderful plays that they made and how they showed improvement since practice or the last game, and remind them of the next practice or game and any other important information. (You could also ask them to think about the game a bit. Just ask them if they had to play the same team tomorrow, what would they do differently, other than win if they lost.) Hold off on any major speech about the game until you have had a chance to sit down and quietly think about the game yourself and discuss it with your coaches. Ask yourself: what could you have done better to prepare the kids? What do you need to work on more in practice? Do you have to switch the players' positions around a bit? When you think you have some ideas about how to prepare for the next practice, start writing them down—that's *your* next practice!

Before you start the next practice, it's a good idea to quickly review with the team the ups and downs of the last game and what you feel you need to improve upon as a team. Then let the kids know that your practice that day will be geared to working on all of your weaknesses, so it's very important for them to concentrate on what they are doing.

At the same time, let the kids know that after a loss (if that was the case), your team either wins or learns. It never loses just because of the score. Tell them that your team is not losers just because the ball took a crazy bounce into the goal, or we accidentally kicked it into our own goal, or because we were just unlucky as five of our shots hit the crossbar. Let them know that they are not losers because you know how hard they have worked at all of the practices and how hard many of them have worked in the off season and how hard they hustle in practices and in the game.

And what did you learn? You may have learned that you need to work harder on your skills and conditioning; you need to play more with your head up; you need to pass the ball with proper pace; you need to slough to the ball more to help out on defense; etc. Explain to your kids that you are very excited about the next game and optimistic about winning as you know that the mistakes the team made were correctable. If you felt that the other team was so much better and you had no chance to win, you would be worried. But you know that if the team corrects its mistakes, it will improve a great deal and play so much better the next game.

SOME CONCLUDING THOUGHTS

If you've read this book from start to finish, we are confident that you have a good solid base on which to build your soccer team. We hope you now have a feel for teaching the fundamentals of the game and helping your players apply them.

If you have used this book as another source of information about soccer, we know you have found some nuggets—some gems—with which to prepare your team more effectively for this wonderful game.

No matter what the reason, we hope you've enjoyed this book and will refer to it often. Soccer has been called "the beautiful game" by the legendary Pelé. We agree and feel that you, too, are beautiful for being part of it.

Good luck, Coach. We've been pleased to help.

GLOSSARY

(Source: *Schools Programme Manual,*
Ontario Soccer Association)

Angle, Narrowing the: When defenders, especially the goalkeeper, move closer to the ball in order to reduce passing or shooting angles.

Cross, Diagonal: Usually played in the offensive third of the field; a ball played forward from right to left or left to right.

Cross, Far Post: A pass made to the goalpost farthest from the point from which the ball was kicked.

Cross, Near Post: A pass made to the goalpost nearest from the point where the ball was kicked.

Defense, Back of: The space between the goalkeeper and the defender nearest to him.

Dribble: Possessing the ball with short touches of the feet.

Driving: Running with the ball by pushing it ahead into spaces and moving after it.

Dummy: When the receiver of a pass feints touching the ball and lets it run by him to a teammate running behind.

Feint: A fake; can be applied to kicking or moving.

Flight: The trajectory of the ball.

Goal side of the ball: The defensive player's position between the player he is marking and the goal he is defending.

Instep: The upper surface of the foot; the laces.

Lofted drive: A powerful kick with the instep driving through the bottom half of the ball.

Marking man-to-man: Defense that requires each of your players to play man-to-man against an opponent.

Neutral Player: One who plays for both teams in a drill.

Pass, Chip: A pass made by stabbing at the bottom of the ball, causing it to go in the air with backspin.

Pass, Flick: A pass made by an outward rotation of the kicking foot, causing contact with the outside of the foot.

Pass, Push: The most used pass in soccer. Ball is struck with the inside of the foot.

Pass, Volley: A pass made by making contact with the ball before it hits the ground.

Pass, Wall: A pass between two players where the receiver passes the ball right back to the passer at a similar angle at which he received it.

Play, Take-over: Crossing motion by two attacking players in which they exchange the ball with the same foot.

Play, One-touch: Passing the ball without first controlling it.

Player, Supporting: Usually a teammate behind the ball, in a position to receive a pass.

Receiving: Controlling the ball by withdrawing the surface used to make contact with it.

Redirecting: Altering the angle and flight of the ball in one movement.

Run, Overlap: The movement of an attacking player from a position behind the ball, around the player with the ball, to a position ahead of the ball.

Space, Creating: Increasing distance between yourself and a teammate, to the side, in front of, or behind opponents.

Tackle: A challenge to win the ball from an opponent.

Thirds of the field: Roughly 35-yard sections of the field. Thirds are designated the defending, the middle, and the attacking.

Turning an opponent: Causing an opponent to turn because you have either played the ball past him or run past him.

Turning with the ball: The act of receiving the ball when facing your goal, then turning with the ball to face the opponent's goal.

GENERAL RESOURCES

Many of the drills and skill descriptions contained herein derive from other coaches and books. Further resources containing information about coaching children and soccer follow:

American Coaching Effectiveness Program. Champaign, Illinois: U. of Chicago.

Canadian Soccer Association, Toronto, Canada; Ontario Soccer Association. *Schools Programme Manual. Level I, II, III Coaching Manuals.*

United States Soccer Federation, Colorado Springs, Colorado. *The Official Soccer Book of the USSF:* Walt Chyzowych. *Coaches Manual:* Robert McNulty and Leonard Lucenko.

Soccer Skills and Tactics. Ken Jones and Pat Welton. New York: Crown, 1976.

Winning Soccer. A. Miller and Norm Wingert. Chicago: Regnery, 1975.